MEDICINE

DOCTORS, DEMONS & DRUGS

MIDDLE EAST STUDIES CENTER
PORTLAND STATE UNIVERSITY
P.O. BOX 751
PORTLAND, OR 97207-0751

Series Editor:
David Salariya was born in Dundee, Scotland, where he studied illustration and printmaking, concentrating on book design in his post-graduate year. He later completed a further post-graduate course in art education at Sussex University. He has illustrated a wide range of books on botanical, historical, and mythical subjects. He has designed and created many new series of children's books for publishers in the U.K. and overseas. In 1989, he established his own publishing company, The Salariya Book Company Ltd. He lives in Brighton with his wife, the illustator Shirley Willis.

Author:
Dr. Kathryn Senior is a former biomedical research scientist who studied at Cambridge University for a first degree in pathology and a doctorate in microbiology. After four years in research she joined the world of publishing, working as an editor of children's science books. She has written *The X-ray Picture Book of the Body* for Watts. Dr. Senior is now a free-lance writer and editor living in Berkshire.

Consultant:
Timothy Boon is Curator of Public Health at the Science Museum in London, where he has worked in various capacities for ten years. His interest in the history of science and medicine dates back to his university studies in Leeds, and in London where he specialized in medical history.

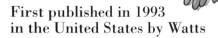

Series Editor	David Salariya
Senior Editor	Ruth Taylor
Book Editor	Vicki Power
Consultant	Timothy Boon
Artists	Mark Bergin
	Ronald Coleman
	Ryz Hajdul
	John James
	Mark Peppé
	Gerald Wood

First published in 1993
in the United States by Watts

Franklin Watts, Inc.
95 Madison Avenue
New York, N.Y. 10016

© The Salariya Book Co Ltd MCMXCIII

Printed in Belgium

Artists
Mark Bergin p 6-7, p 8-9, p 14-15, p 16-17, p 26-27; **Ronald Coleman** p 32-33; **Ryz Hajdul** p 22-23, p 38-39; **John James** p 18-19, p 20-21, p 30-31, p 42-43; **Mark Peppé** p 36-37, p 40-41; **Gerald Wood** p 10-11, p 12-13, p 24-25, p 34-35.

Library of Congress Cataloging-in-Publication Data
Senior, Kathryn,
    Medicine / by Kathryn Senior.
        p. cm. – (Timelines)
    Includes index.
    Summary: Provides a concise overview of the history of medicine, from witch doctors to the latest in prostheses and organ transplant surgery.
    ISBN 0-531-14279-5 (lib. bdg.) — ISBN 0-531-15706-7 (pbk.)
    1. Medicine – History – Juvenile literature. [1. Medicine – History.] I. Title. II. Series: Timelines (Franklin Watts, Inc.)
R133.5.S46 1993
610'.9 – dc20
                                                          93-10608
                                                          CIP AC

TIMELINES
MEDICINE

DOCTORS, DEMONS & DRUGS

Written by
KATHRYN SENIOR

Created & Designed by
DAVID SALARIYA

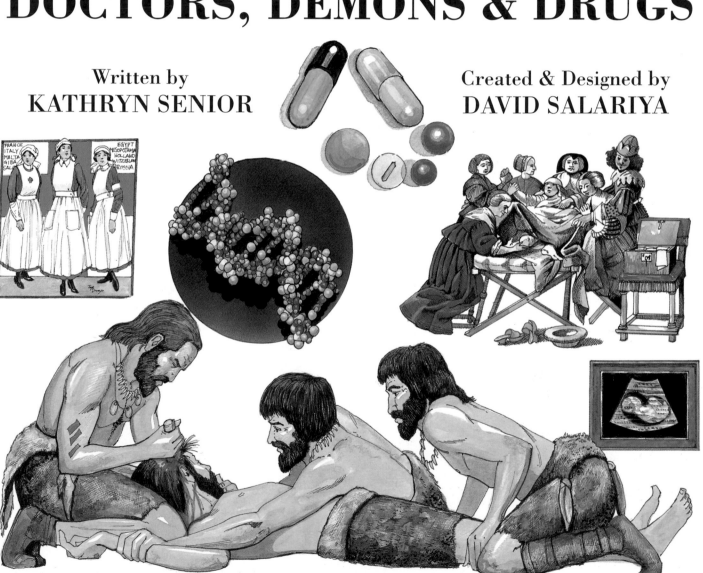

FRANKLIN WATTS

New York • Chicago • London • Toronto • Sydney

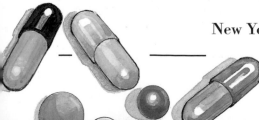
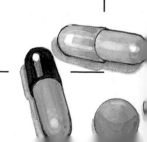

CONTENTS

SYR:
ZINGIB:

G.WOOD

EARLY MEDICINE AND MAGIC

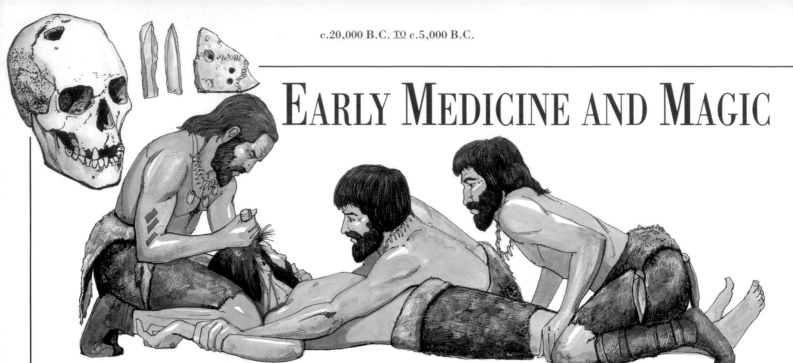

△ TREPANNING, cutting a hole in the skull, was believed to let out evil spirits and so cure an illness. It was a common treatment for headaches. This operation was carried out between c.20,000 B.C. and c.10,000 B.C.

△ A MEDICINE MAN'S KIT – teeth, bells, flints, animal claws, carved sticks, and a lizard skin.

◁ A FETISH used in Zaire to exorcise (drive out) disease-causing spirits. When held in front of the patient, the mirror was believed to absorb illness.

▽ SUSRUTA, a famed Hindu surgeon, treating a noble of ancient India for an ear injury. He constructed an artificial earlobe using strips of flesh from other parts of the man's body.

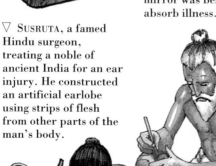

PEOPLE WHO LIVED over 5,000 years ago thought that illness was caused by evil in their bodies. Sickness was a punishment from the gods or from spirits for doing something wrong. Magic and witchcraft were practiced in many ancient tribes. Charms and spells and images of gods or even of the sick person were used to drive the disease away. People in the earliest civilizations also began to use simple herbal remedies. They learned, probably by trial and error, which herbs would best cure a stomachache or fever.

▽▷ SANDPAINTING ceremonies – an important part of Navaho medicine.

The medicine man or witch doctor was the central figure in tribal medicine and often the most important man in the village. He would treat everyone in the tribe with magic and simple herbal remedies. This type of medicine existed in many cultures. Ancient peoples may have used magic and herbs in the same way as North American Indians did a hundred years ago and as some tribal peoples still do today.

Ancient Mesopotamians believed in a spectrum of illness. At opposite ends of the spectrum were illnesses caused by evil spirits and illnesses caused by physical problems, such as worms. A medicine man decided at which end of the spectrum the illness lay and then sent the patient to an exorcist (to drive away the evil spirit) or to an herbalist (for an herbal mixture to kill the worms).

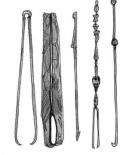

△ METAL surgical instruments used 4,500 years ago in Mesopotamia.

◁ MUMMIFICATION preserved the bodies of Egyptians for the afterlife.

▽ ORGANS of the dead person were removed and preserved separately in clay jars.

△ MESOPOTAMIAN medicine was regulated by the Code of Hammurabi. *Above*, a physician defends himself against the complaints of a dissatisfied patient.

Although Egyptians who were ill relied on their gods for healing, their medicine was quite sophisticated. Egyptian doctors carried out minor operations and treated many ailments, including scorpion bites. They sucked blood from the wound and then bound the affected limb to keep the poison from spreading. Egyptians may have learned more about the body from the process of mummification. Preparing the dead for burial involved cutting the body open and seeing the effects of disease.

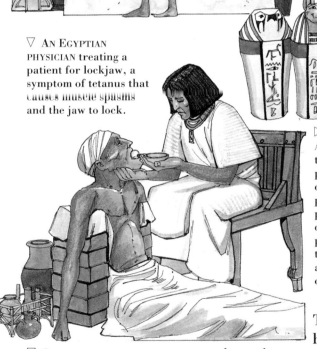

▽ AN EGYPTIAN PHYSICIAN treating a patient for lockjaw, a symptom of tetanus that causes muscle spasms and the jaw to lock.

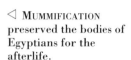

▷ A CHINESE ACUPUNCTURE MAP of the ear, showing the points where needles can be inserted. Some points can give rapid pain relief. It has been claimed that several points have been used to give complete anesthesia for an operation.

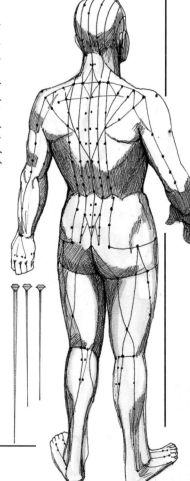

The ancient Chinese believed that the body was ruled by two forces, light and dark, or yin and yang. When one force overcame the other, the body's balance was upset and the person became ill. By inserting fine needles into the body, an acupuncturist would stimulate either yin or yang, to re-establish a balance. Yin or yang were thought to flow through channels in the body, which were illustrated on maps. This continues to be the philosophy behind acupuncture today.

▽ OVER THE CENTURIES, many Egyptian mummies were ground up and used as medicine.

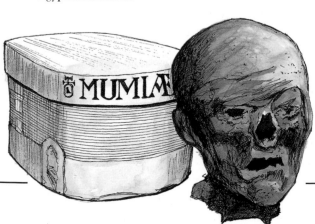

THE GREEKS

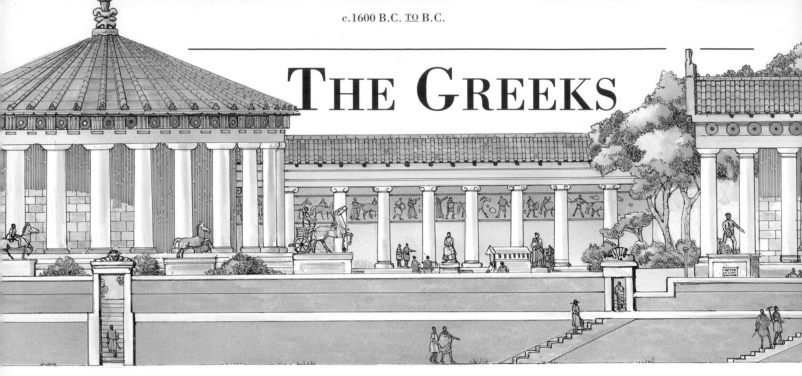

△ GREEKS DOCTORS tried to find out what was wrong with their patients by observation and examination.

△ DOCTORS thought that bloodletting helped to restore the balance of the humors.

▽ THESE FIGURES (c.300 B.C.) show typical outward signs of different illnesses. Trainee doctors studied them.

GREEK MEDICINE showed a great deal of sophistication compared with the tribal medicine of primitive cultures. The Greeks saw health as an ideal to be pursued.

The most important contribution made by the ancient Greeks was formulated by the philosopher Hippocrates (c.460 - 377 B.C.), and formed the basis of medical theory for the next two thousand years. The Greeks believed that the body contained four "humors" – blood, phlegm, yellow bile and black bile. An imbalance of these humors resulted in disease, so doctors tried to restore the balance by methods that included bloodletting, purging, baths, and special diets.

Hippocrates and his followers freed medicine from the superstition that had dominated it for centuries. They encouraged doctors to develop a good bedside manner, to observe patients carefully, and they set guidelines for surgery, which was common. Their theories were widely used until the rise of modern scientific medicine in the nineteenth century.

△ THE SANCTUARY of Asclepius at Epidaurus, a famous center of healing in ancient Greece dating from the 6th century B.C. Asclepius was the god of healing. Excavated ruins show there were baths, hostels, a library, a theater, a gymnasium, and temples.

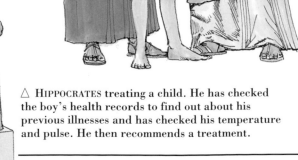

△ HIPPOCRATES treating a child. He has checked the boy's health records to find out about his previous illnesses and has checked his temperature and pulse. He then recommends a treatment.

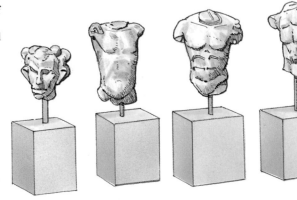

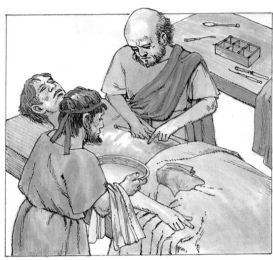

◁ SOME GREEK
DOCTORS learned how
the human body
worked by studying
bodies of dead people.

△ GREEK surgical
instruments.

△ GREEK FUNERALS
were full of rituals.
Above, relatives of the
dead man wash and
dress the corpse.

▽ When followers of
the cult of Asclepius,
the Greek god of
healing, were ill, they
would go to one of his
temples to sleep. They believed
that the god visited them during
dreams to heal them or to tell
them what treatment they
should have. Those who were
cured showed their thanks by
hanging votive offerings (small
stone images) on the wall of the
temple. More than 200
temples existed between
500 B.C. and A.D. 500.

▷ THIS
STATUE of
Asclepius
shows him
holding a
stick
entwined
with his
symbol, a
serpent.
Serpents
were thought
to possess
healing
powers.

Aristotle (384-322 B.C.) was another
great figure in Greek medicine. He was
a philosopher who taught that medicine
should be based on an understanding
of science. He argued that this could
only be done by direct investigation.
Anatomy (the structure of the body)
and physiology (how the body works)
were studied for the first time by
dissecting dead bodies. His
observations of how a baby develops in
its mother's body were particularly
detailed. He had many followers and
his influence lasted for many
generations.

Rosemary.

Sage.

THE ROMANS

ROMAN MEDICINE was very similar to that of the Greeks; most of the doctors were Greek and many of the herbal remedies and healing rituals were the same. The Romans still relied heavily on the intervention of their gods when someone became sick. The Romans were quite healthy people. They had some effective drugs, mostly based on herbs and plants, and they paid special attention to hygiene. They bathed and washed themselves regularly and kept their homes and towns clean and neat. They had an advanced system to supply fresh, clean water and built latrines and sewage systems so sophisticated that they rivaled those that existed in Britain only one hundred years ago.

The most important doctor in Roman medicine was called Galen (A.D. 129-199). His reputation as a great physician grew when he became the emperor's doctor, but he was an unpopular man, hated by his colleagues. After being forced to leave Rome in A.D. 166 he later returned because of a great plague. He was allowed to stay after this and began to write down his opinions on how medicine should be practiced.

△ A CHEMISTS'S SHOP in Roman Gaul (now France). The Romans used many plants as medicines.

△ THE ROMANS burned (cremated) their dead. The ashes were put into marble or glass urns and then placed in family tombs or cemeteries.

Elecampane

Fennel

Garlic

△ ROMAN DOCTORS used various herbs for different illnesses. Elecampane was used to aid digestion, fennel was a calming herb, and other herbs were used as anesthetics.

▽ GALEN is treating a patient using cupping. Small cups, heated by the lamp, are placed over small cuts in the boy's skin. As the air in the cup cools down it takes up less space and blood from the cuts is sucked out. Galen did this to draw poisons out of the body.

◁ A ROMAN DOCTOR carefully examines a patient. The man, who is extremely thin and obviously ill, is having his pulse taken.

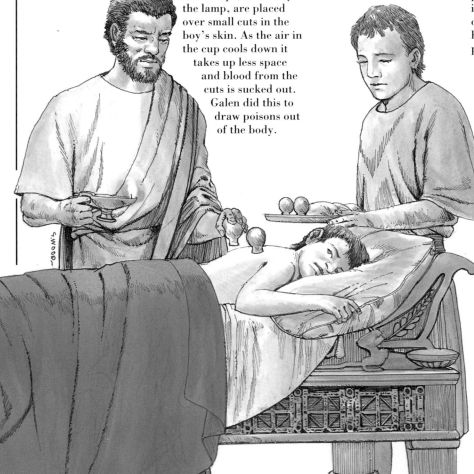

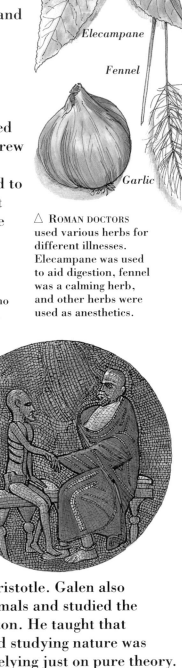

Galen's work was based on the writings of Aristotle. Galen also dissected animals and studied the human skeleton. He taught that observing and studying nature was better than relying just on pure theory. His writings were accepted as the basis of medicine for more than 1,500 years after his death.

△ THE HOSPITAL had an operating theater, patients' rooms, latrines, baths, and storerooms, arranged around a courtyard.

▽ A ROMAN SURGEON at work. Operations were a painful and dangerous part of Roman medicine and few patients survived.

△ A ROMAN fort hospital, excavated at Housesteads, in present- day England. The hospital probably provided treatment for several local forts.

The main sewage system was in operation in Rome in the sixth century B.C. Aqueducts were built later to provide the city with fresh water. Public baths and places to exercise were built throughout the Roman empire. Such hygiene measures controlled the spread of disease very well. For those who did become ill, Roman hospitals were also advanced. One excavated in Germany had a corridor design that was later adopted by Florence Nightingale. But the Romans could not treat serious illness effectively; patients who needed surgery or who were very ill with an infection usually died.

◁ To KEEP CLEAN, Romans rubbed oil on their skin and scraped it off with a strigil.

▽ THE ROMANS did not go to the baths just to get clean; they also went for exercise, games, relaxation, and socializing.

△ ROMAN MEDICAL INSTRUMENTS (*top to bottom*): handsaw, tweezers, forceps, speculum for internal examinations, and a spatula.

▽ SANITATION, which included clean running water, helped to control the spread of infection and disease in Roman settlements.

ISLAMIC MEDICINE

AS THE ROMAN EMPIRE began to collapse and
Europe plunged into the Dark Ages, Islamic
civilization flourished. The Arabs gathered medical
knowledge and passed it on through the generations.
Rhazes, a well-known Arab doctor (A.D. c.865-925), became the
head physician in Baghdad. When asked to choose the site
of a new hospital in Baghdad, he hung a dead animal at
each of the four corners of the city to see which one decayed
the most slowly. Rhazes concluded that this area was likely
to be the cleanest and therefore the most suitable for the
hospital. He was also the first doctor to
be able to tell the difference between
smallpox and measles.

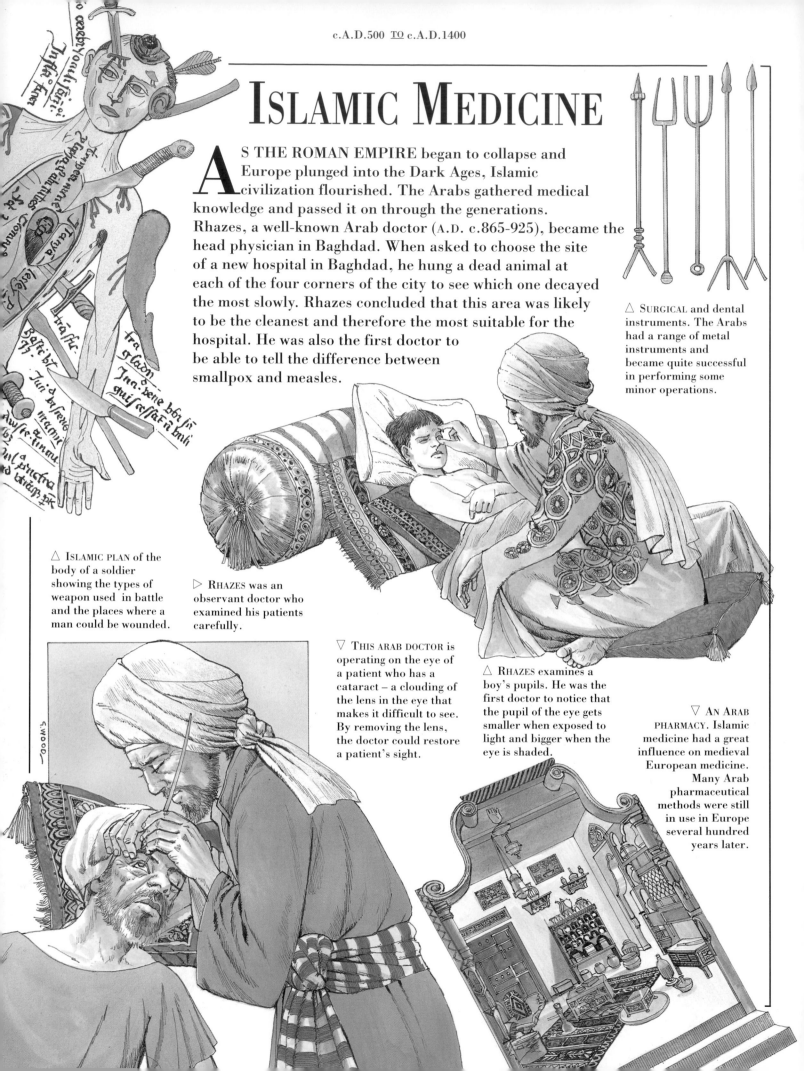

△ SURGICAL and dental
instruments. The Arabs
had a range of metal
instruments and
became quite successful
in performing some
minor operations.

△ ISLAMIC PLAN of the
body of a soldier
showing the types of
weapon used in battle
and the places where a
man could be wounded.

▷ RHAZES was an
observant doctor who
examined his patients
carefully.

▽ THIS ARAB DOCTOR is
operating on the eye of
a patient who has a
cataract – a clouding of
the lens in the eye that
makes it difficult to see.
By removing the lens,
the doctor could restore
a patient's sight.

△ RHAZES examines a
boy's pupils. He was the
first doctor to notice that
the pupil of the eye gets
smaller when exposed to
light and bigger when the
eye is shaded.

▽ AN ARAB
PHARMACY. Islamic
medicine had a great
influence on medieval
European medicine.
Many Arab
pharmaceutical
methods were still
in use in Europe
several hundred
years later.

THE DARK AGES

BY THE MIDDLE of the third century A.D. the Roman Empire was so big that it could not be ruled by one man. This made the Empire vulnerable and it broke up when attacked by nomadic armies in the fifth century. The Anglo-Saxons, the Huns, the Vandals, and the Goths overran many parts of the world and this brought about a period in Europe known as the Dark Ages. The Romans' knowledge and civilization were lost. The invaders did not build sophisticated towns and living conditions became poor. Medical knowledge did not advance in Europe for almost a thousand years.

Religion had a great influence on medicine during the Dark Ages. It was the doctor's job to drive away evil, rather than to find the cause of an illness. The early Christian Church taught people that disease was a punishment from God. People were told to pray to the saints if they wanted to be healed. Many sick people made pilgrimages to the shrines of dead saints in the hope that touching the relics would cure them.

△ DOCTORS in the Dark Ages usually prescribed an herbal remedy and a magic spell.

△ SIMPLE HERBAL REMEDIES were often mixtures to make the patient vomit or pastes to put on a wound.

△ AT THE END of the Dark Ages, doctors became more interested in how the body worked.

△ EXAMINING THE URINE played an important part in diagnosing illness.

▽ COSMAS AND DAMIAN were mythical twin doctors who were made saints and prayed to for medical knowledge.

▽ A SCENE from a painting showing an imaginary operation. The twins clean their instruments after grafting the leg of a Moor (a black North African) onto a white man.

△ UROSCOPY CHART.
The process of
examining the urine
became more
sophisticated during the
12th and 13th
centuries.

△ STUDENTS TREAT
PATIENTS at Salerno,
site of the first medical
school, founded in the
late 10th century.

△ A PATIENT is bled
(*above center*) and his
urine examined, both
common treatments of
the Middle Ages.

PLAGUE

IN THE MIDDLE AGES the
teaching of medicine became better
organized. Medical knowledge from
the Greeks and Romans and also from
the Arabs was collected by monks,
and medical schools began
to flourish.

Great epidemics affected many people
during the Middle Ages. As well as the
plague, leprosy was also common in
Europe. An early medical writer,
Gilbertus Anglicus, noted that when
people got leprosy their eyebrows and
eyelashes fell off, their faces became
thick and lumpy, and their arms and
legs were eaten away.

*A leper's
begging bowl.*

Clappers.

▷ LEPERS WERE FORCED
to carry clappers to warn
people that they were near.

▷ LEPERS were
outcasts in medieval
Europe. In 1313, Phillip
the Fair ordered all
lepers in France
to be
burned.

▽ PRIESTS opened hostels
for lepers in the 13th
century. The lepers lived
apart from unaffected
people. Leprosy had finally
disappeared from Europe by
the 16th century.

▽ The plague was
caused by bacteria that
bred in rats. It was
spread by the plague
flea which sucked a
rat's blood and then
jumped off to suck
human blood.

◁△ THE PLAGUE began
in 1334 and in less than
20 years killed three-
quarters of the
populations of Europe
and Asia.

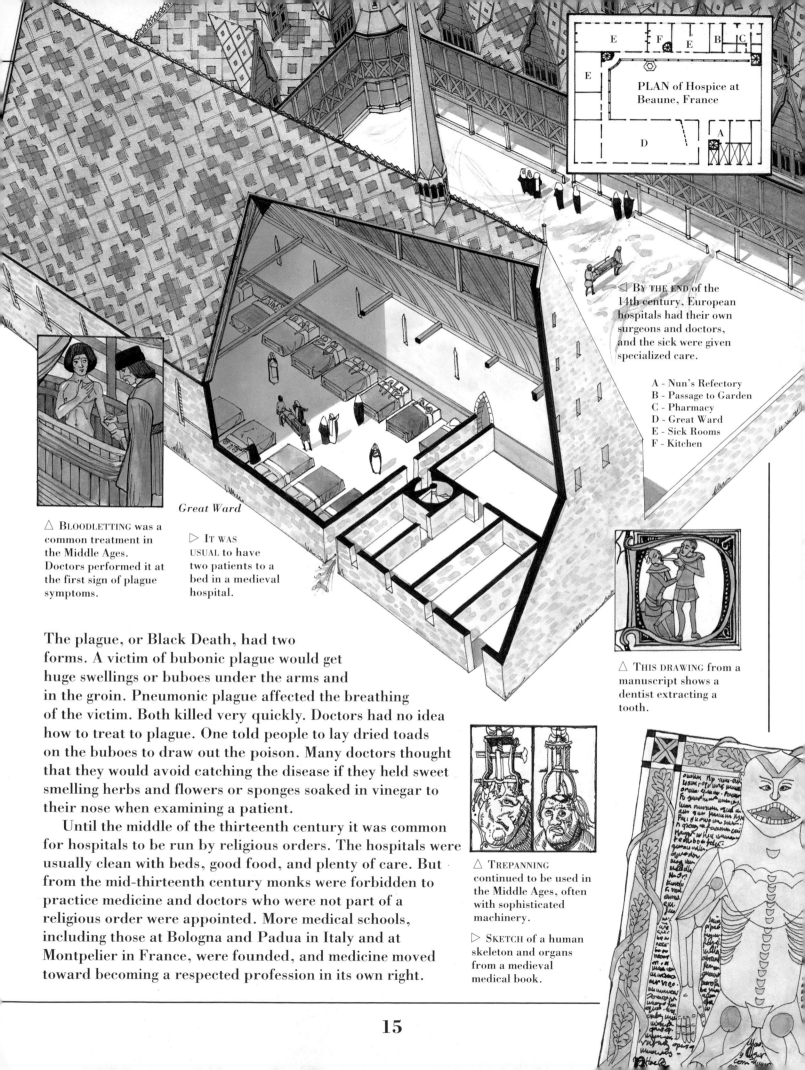

PLAN of Hospice at Beaune, France

▽ BY THE END of the 14th century, European hospitals had their own surgeons and doctors, and the sick were given specialized care.

A - Nun's Refectory
B - Passage to Garden
C - Pharmacy
D - Great Ward
E - Sick Rooms
F - Kitchen

Great Ward

△ BLOODLETTING was a common treatment in the Middle Ages. Doctors performed it at the first sign of plague symptoms.

▷ IT WAS USUAL to have two patients to a bed in a medieval hospital.

△ THIS DRAWING from a manuscript shows a dentist extracting a tooth.

The plague, or Black Death, had two forms. A victim of bubonic plague would get huge swellings or buboes under the arms and in the groin. Pneumonic plague affected the breathing of the victim. Both killed very quickly. Doctors had no idea how to treat to plague. One told people to lay dried toads on the buboes to draw out the poison. Many doctors thought that they would avoid catching the disease if they held sweet smelling herbs and flowers or sponges soaked in vinegar to their nose when examining a patient.

Until the middle of the thirteenth century it was common for hospitals to be run by religious orders. The hospitals were usually clean with beds, good food, and plenty of care. But from the mid-thirteenth century monks were forbidden to practice medicine and doctors who were not part of a religious order were appointed. More medical schools, including those at Bologna and Padua in Italy and at Montpelier in France, were founded, and medicine moved toward becoming a respected profession in its own right.

△ TREPANNING continued to be used in the Middle Ages, often with sophisticated machinery.

▷ SKETCH of a human skeleton and organs from a medieval medical book.

THE RENAISSANCE

RENAISSANCE means rebirth and this period in history involved a rebirth of people's interest in learning and in the world around them. It began in Italy at the end of the fourteenth century and spread throughout Europe, reaching its peak almost 200 years later. People began to be interested in science and in how their bodies worked. Galileo (1564-1642) invented the thermometer, although thermometers were not widely used until the nineteenth century. Doctors continued to follow the Greek theory that the body contained four types of fluid – blood, phlegm, yellow bile, and black bile. When the fluids were not well-balanced, illness resulted. Doctors tried to detect such imbalances and put them right.

▽ STUDENTS at a lecture in the anatomy theater in Padua, Italy.

Lecturer.

Dissector.

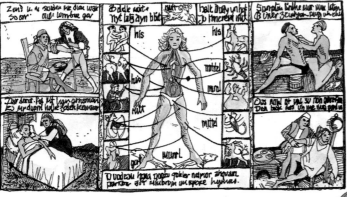

△ Calendar (*center*) showing the seasons when it was good to carry out bloodletting. The scenes at the sides show bleeding (*top left*), cupping (*bottom left*), giving medicine (*top right*) and feeling the pulse (*bottom right*).

The increased use of gunpowder supplied surgeons with many casualties and surgery improved with practice. Gaspare Tagliacozzi (1540-1599) of Italy transplanted skin from a patient's arm onto his nose.

◁ VESALIUS was a great anatomist but his ideas caused bad feeling because they disagreed with the views of Galen, which had lasted since Roman times.

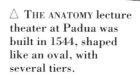

Curiosity about the human body led to more dissections of corpses. Andreas Vesalius (1514-1564) was the most famous anatomist of his time. He trained as a doctor in Paris and became professor of surgery and anatomy at Padua University. Padua had a famous anatomy lecture theater – because of its design, students were never more than thirty feet from the dissection table.

Vesalius drew the human body in action to show how it worked as well as how it was structured. He contradicted many of the old ideas that had been put forward by Galen. Vesalius wrote a book, *De humani corporis fabrica libri septum* (*Seven Books on the Structure of the Human Body*), published in 1543, which showed the results of his dissection and study of the human body. The publication of this series marked the beginning of scientific anatomy.

△ THE ANATOMY lecture theater at Padua was built in 1544, shaped like an oval, with several tiers.

▽ VESALIUS'S book contained remarkable anatomical illustrations from woodcuts by Jan Stephan von Calcar.

△ THIS PATIENT, who has a broken arm, is being treated by a form of traction. The man on the right is stretching the broken limb to straighten it as it heals. The principle behind the treatment remains the same today.

△ THE CONTENTS of a surgeon's medical chest from the English ship Mary Rose, which sank in 1545. These included syringes, medicine bottles, and scales for weighing medical powders, as well as bowls and flasks.

△ 15TH-CENTURY WOOD CARVING showing treatment for piles.

△ SURGERY improved during the Renaissance but amputating a leg was still an horrific and painful operation.

△ LARGE SYRINGES were also found. These were probably used to treat sexually transmitted diseases, which were common in sailors.

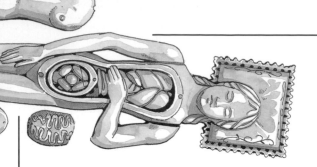

16TH & 17TH CENTURIES

AFTER THE RENAISSANCE the European center of excellence in medical teaching moved from Padua in Italy to Leyden in Holland during the seventeenth century. William Harvey, an English doctor (1578-1657), made an exciting discovery. Until then it had been thought that blood flowed from the heart to the extremities and back again, but Harvey showed that blood circulated around the body. Later, doctors discovered that circulation was driven by a pump – the heart.

△ ANATOMICAL model from 16th-century Italy. The organs can be seen by taking off the front of the body.

△ A HUNGARIAN MEDICAL BOOK showing how cauterizing irons were used. The irons (*in front*) were heated to burn and seal a wound.

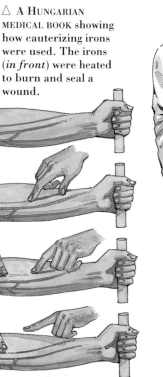

△ ▷ HARVEY showed that the flow of blood to the heart can be stopped by pressing on a vein. If a second finger presses on the vein higher up and the first finger is released, blood starts flowing through the empty portion of the vein.

△ ANATOMY LECTURE THEATER, Leyden, Holland. Pieter Paaw, professor of anatomy, is dissecting a corpse.

△ THOMAS SYDENHAM (1624-1689). He was called the "Father of Clinical Medicine" in Britain.

△ AN ENGRAVING by Abraham Bosse (1602-1676) showing a 17th-century doctor of French middle-class society visiting a patient. He is about to give the patient an enema. He has a syringe, probably full of warm water, which he will insert into her rectum. She is attended by her maids – on the left, one of them brings in a commode.

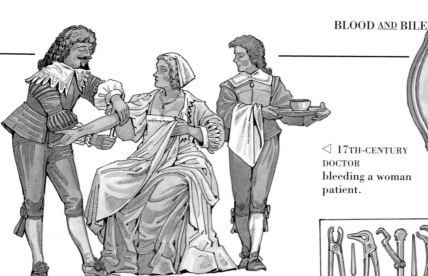

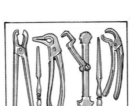

◁ 17TH-CENTURY DOCTOR bleeding a woman patient.

△ BLOODLETTING INSTRUMENTS – bowl, armband, knives, and vein openers used in the 17th century.

◁ DENTAL FORCEPS – to pull out, cut, and file teeth.

The Swiss doctor Paracelsus (c.1493-1541) dismissed contemporary medical theories. He experimented with chemicals and encouraged doctors to use them to treat illnesses. Most doctors continued to treat patients by regulating the humors using bloodletting and purging.

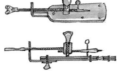

△ ▷ VAN LEEUWENHOEK'S MICROSCOPE was held up to the eye.

△ VAN LEEUWENHOEK'S DRAWINGS of bacteria from his own mouth as seen under his microscope in 1683. He called them "little animals" and thought that they moved very gracefully.

△ REMBRANDT, the Dutch painter, is shown painting *A Lesson in Anatomy by Doctor Tulp* in 1632. The artist was commissioned to record the public dissection of the arm of an executed criminal.

◁ MICROSCOPES built by the Englishman Robert Hooke, 1665.

Anton van Leeuwenhoek (1632-1723) was a merchant from Delft in Holland who devoted himself to studying life under the microscope. He made over 200 microscopes and although the magnifications he managed to achieve were no more than 160 times, he made some valuable observations. He described the compound eye of the fly and the capillaries in the tail of a tadpole. He was also the first scientist to find that red blood cells were oval in fish and frogs but round in mammals.

THE 18TH CENTURY

1. AN 18TH-CENTURY MEDICAL STUDENT in Edinburgh would begin his day at 7 a.m. by reading textbooks.

2. He would attend a chemistry lecture and take as many notes as possible.

EARLY IN THE 18TH CENTURY the center for medical education in Europe moved from Leyden, in Holland, to Scotland. A school of medicine was established at Edinburgh in 1726, and Alexander Monro was appointed Professor of Anatomy there.

3. At 9:30 a.m. he would have breakfast – if he were poor he would probably eat porridge and milk.

4. At 10 a.m. he might write out his scribbled notes so that he could read them later.

5. At 12 noon he would visit wards in the Edinburgh Royal Infirmary.

△ THE CHARITY BOX was used to collect money for the hospital in its early days.

The system of medical training at Edinburgh was thorough and the school was expanded. Alexander Monro was followed as professor of anatomy by his son and then his grandson (both also called Alexander). The first two Monros were excellent lecturers, but Alexander III was considered by some to be a poor anatomist.

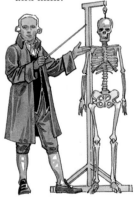

6. At 1 p.m. he would go to an anatomy lecture given by one of the famous Monro professors.

7. At 3 p.m. he would go home for a dinner of potato and herring. Sometimes it was just bread and milk.

8. At 4 p.m. he would attend an hour-long lecture on midwifery.

△ THE MONRO FAMILY was a dominant force at the Edinburgh Medical School for over 120 years. Father, son, and grandson were all Professors of Anatomy between 1726 and 1846.

9. He would write out his notes again so he could read them at exam time.

10. He would attend another anatomy lesson at 6 p.m. Sometimes he and his fellow students managed to fit in a drink at the local inn after evening lectures.

11. At 9 p.m. he would go home for a supper of bread and milk (left).

12. He would study late into the evening and go to bed at midnight (right).

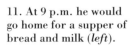

▽ A TICKET for the anatomy class of Alexander Monro II in 1785.

△ JAMES LIND (1716-1794) discovered that scurvy could be cured in sailors by giving them lemons and limes.

As more students studied medicine, more bodies were needed for dissection. Doctors were allowed to use only the bodies of criminals, so a shortage of bodies occurred. Soon the widespread practice of "body snatching" grew up to satisfy the demands of the Edinburgh anatomists. Body snatchers dug up fresh graves and sold the corpes to the medical school. Public outrage grew over the issue.

▽ FUNERALS were carefully watched by body snatchers, who sometimes returned at night to steal the body.

△ BODY SNATCHERS were able to steal a body from a 6-foot (2-m) deep grave in an hour. They dug down to the head end of the coffin, then used iron hooks to pull off the lid, and hauled out the body.

▽ DRAWINGS of Burke and Hare at their trial in 1828.

▽ MORTSAFES – iron cases with railings on top of the grave were used to deter body snatchers.

△ A SAW used in surgery in the 18th century. Large saws were used to speed up amputations.

△ IN 1828 Robert Penman had a tumor (14 inches/38cm across) removed from his mouth.

◁ BRITISH WOMEN were not allowed to graduate from medical school until 1876. Dr James Barry, a respected doctor who had graduated from Edinburgh in 1812, was discovered upon "his" death in 1865 to be a woman.

◁ A MOORE'S CLAMP compressed the nerves for pain relief during an amputation.

△ JAMES YOUNG SIMPSON (1811-1870) first used chloroform as an anesthetic for women in childbirth. He gave it to Queen Victoria during the birth of her 7th child.

The money offered by the anatomists for corpses motivated two Irishmen, Burke and Hare, to murder sixteen people. After being discovered in November 1828, Hare gave evidence against Burke and escaped execution, but Burke was hanged in public. In 1832 the government passed the Anatomy Act, which allowed anatomists to obtain unclaimed bodies from hospitals and workhouses, and body snatching died out.

Smallpox was rampant in the 18th century. Over 60 million people died in Europe. In 1796, a vaccination for smallpox was intoduced by the English doctor Edward Jenner. He noticed that milkmaids who often got a mild disease called cowpox never caught smallpox. He began to give people fluid from a cowpox sore. Vaccination was successful and later became compulsory. It finally stamped the disease out completely in the the 1970s.

▷ DOCTORS originally tried to protect people from smallpox by making a cut in a patient's arm and then drawing a thread through it that had been soaked in fluid from a smallpox sore. But the patients often caught smallpox and died. Jenner did the same thing but with fluid from a cowpox sore and this prevented patients from getting smallpox.

▷ A 19TH-CENTURY CARTOON implying that people given the cowpox vaccine might gain the features of cows.

▽ 19TH-CENTURY VACCINATION KIT, with sharp blades to pierce the patient's skin.

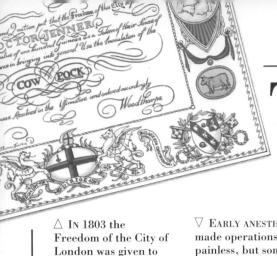

THE SCIENTISTS

△ FRENCH DOCTOR René Laënnec invented the stethoscope in 1816.

THE NINETEENTH CENTURY saw a revolution in medicine, with many scientific discoveries being made. Surgeons carried out a wider range of operations than ever. Ether was first used in the United States in 1842, and in 1846 Peter Squire gave ether anesthetic to a patient while his leg was being amputated. The patient remained unconscious throughout and felt no pain. Later in the nineteenth century the work of three medical scientists – Louis Pasteur, Robert Koch, and Joseph Lister – led to the discovery that bacteria were the cause of infection in wounds after an operation. By the end of the century operations were carried out in clean conditions and carbolic acid was sprayed onto the wound during and after surgery. More people began to survive operations.

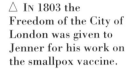

△ IN 1803 the Freedom of the City of London was given to Jenner for his work on the smallpox vaccine.

▽ EARLY ANESTHETICS made operations painless, but some patients died when they were given too much.

△ APPARATUS used to give anesthetics.

△ ANESTHETICS, first used in 1824, and antiseptics, discovered in 1865, revolutionized surgery.

▽ Louis Pasteur (1822-1895) was a remarkable medical scientist. He showed that airborne bacteria were the cause of decay and disease, leading the way for development of antiseptic surgery. He developed vaccines and invented pasteurization – heating milk and beer to destroy harmful bacteria.

△ ROBERT KOCH (1843-1910) showed that many infections were caused by bacteria.

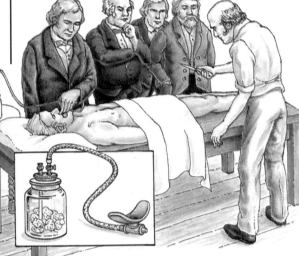

◁ LISTER operates on a patient in 1880. The carbolic spray is on a table close to the operating table and is being directed into position by an assistant. Later more effective disinfectants were used and all instruments were sterilized by steam.

△ EMILE ROUX (1853-1933), a brilliant doctor who worked with Pasteur from 1880.

△ JOSEPH LISTER (1827-1912) studied in London and Edinburgh.

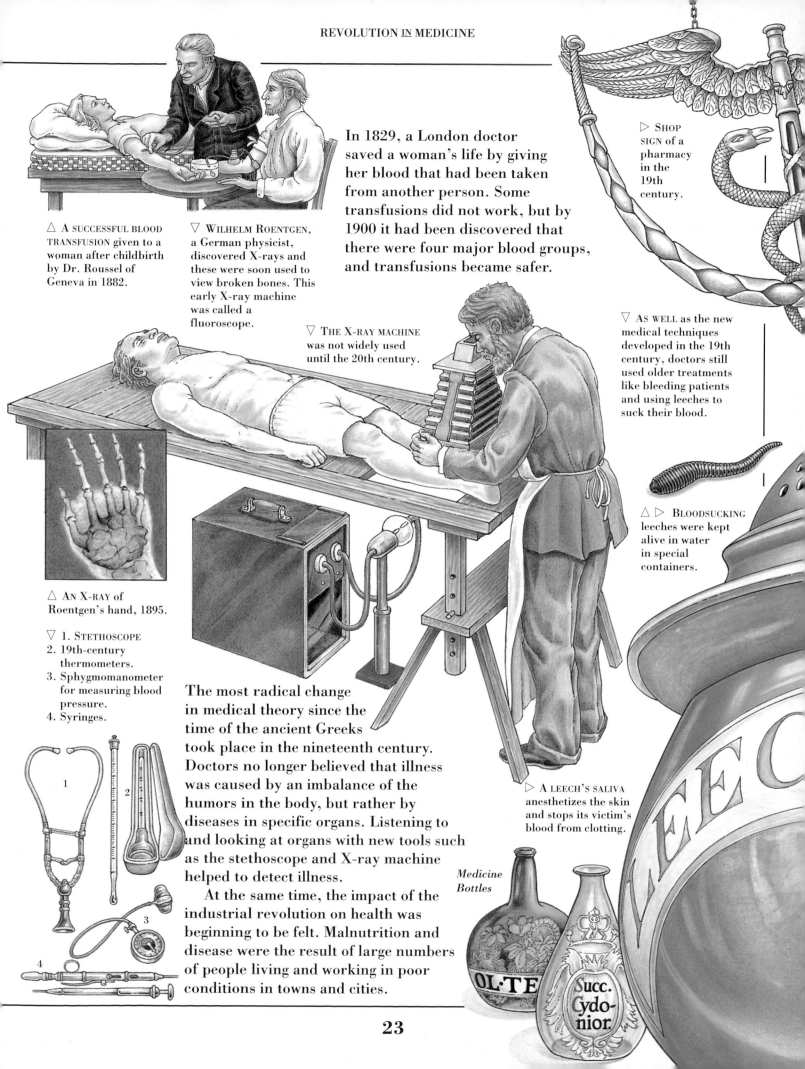

△ A SUCCESSFUL BLOOD TRANSFUSION given to a woman after childbirth by Dr. Roussel of Geneva in 1882.

▽ WILHELM ROENTGEN, a German physicist, discovered X-rays and these were soon used to view broken bones. This early X-ray machine was called a fluoroscope.

In 1829, a London doctor saved a woman's life by giving her blood that had been taken from another person. Some transfusions did not work, but by 1900 it had been discovered that there were four major blood groups, and transfusions became safer.

▷ SHOP SIGN of a pharmacy in the 19th century.

▽ THE X-RAY MACHINE was not widely used until the 20th century.

▽ AS WELL as the new medical techniques developed in the 19th century, doctors still used older treatments like bleeding patients and using leeches to suck their blood.

△ AN X-RAY of Roentgen's hand, 1895.

△▷ BLOODSUCKING leeches were kept alive in water in special containers.

▽ 1. STETHOSCOPE
2. 19th-century thermometers.
3. Sphygmomanometer for measuring blood pressure.
4. Syringes.

The most radical change in medical theory since the time of the ancient Greeks took place in the nineteenth century. Doctors no longer believed that illness was caused by an imbalance of the humors in the body, but rather by diseases in specific organs. Listening to and looking at organs with new tools such as the stethoscope and X-ray machine helped to detect illness.

At the same time, the impact of the industrial revolution on health was beginning to be felt. Malnutrition and disease were the result of large numbers of people living and working in poor conditions in towns and cities.

▷ A LEECH'S SALIVA anesthetizes the skin and stops its victim's blood from clotting.

Medicine Bottles

Succ. Cydo-nior.

MENTAL HEALTH

△ MANY MEDIEVAL MANUSCRIPTS of the Psalms are decorated with drawings of fools and madmen.

THE TREATMENT OF MENTAL ILLNESS throughout the ages has been tinged with prejudice and fear. It has been thought that the mentally ill were possessed by evil spirits, and sometimes they have been tortured and imprisoned. Over the centuries doctors have tried to explain the causes of mental illness – the ancient Greeks believed it to be caused by an imbalance of the four humors, for example. But the scientific discoveries about disease in the seventeenth and eighteenth centuries did not lead to a better understanding of mental illness. Asylums were built in which to confine the mentally ill. There, patients were sometimes chained up or treated with bizarre mechanical contraptions, such as whirling cages. During this time, some doctors were advocating a more gentle approach to treating the mentally ill.

△ THIS 1536 DRAWING shows how anatomists tried to relate brain functions to specific points in the brain.

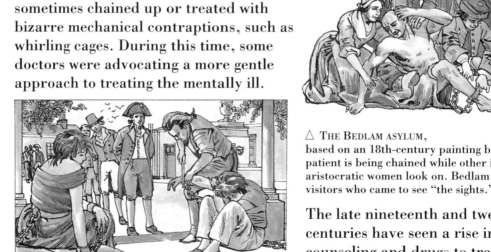

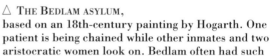

△ A 17TH-CENTURY DUTCH SCULPTURE entitled *The Woman from the Madhouse*.

△ THE BEDLAM ASYLUM, based on an 18th-century painting by Hogarth. One patient is being chained while other inmates and two aristocratic women look on. Bedlam often had such visitors who came to see "the sights."

The late nineteenth and twentieth centuries have seen a rise in the use of counseling and drugs to treat the mentally disturbed, as well as a better understanding of the genetic causes of mental illness. Efforts are now made to encourage the mentally ill to live and work in the community.

△ BENJAMIN RUSH (1745-1813), father of American psychiatry.

△ THE TREATMENT OF THE INSANE started to improve in the 18th century, because of the work of Dr. Philippe Pinel in France. Pinel insisted that patients should be unchained and treated in a more humane way.

▽ MODERN PSYCHIATRIC TREATMENT includes careful counseling by trained professionals.

△ A BED that whirled around and around was a 19th-century treatment for madness.

△ WATER TREATMENT involved repeatedly dousing the patient with cold water.

◁ SIGMUND FREUD (1856-1939), Austrian physician who founded psychoanalysis, a treatment for mental illness. His work was very influential.

△ WILLIAM MORRIS, who was chained to an upright post in Bedlam for 12 years. When his case was made public, moves were made to reform asylums.

DENTISTRY

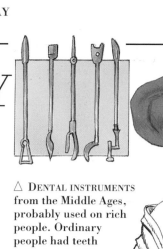

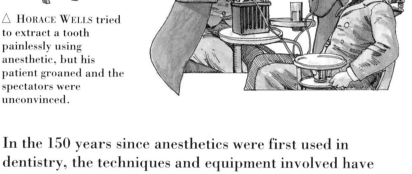 FALSE TEETH were used as early as 700 B.C. by the Etruscan people. They used human or animal teeth and bound them to real teeth with gold wire.

DENTISTRY did not become a profession until the nineteenth century. Some ancient civilizations such as the Etruscans made simple dentures, but until anesthetics were first used in the 1840s, rotten teeth were removed with pliers with no attempt to lessen the pain. Tooth decay was widespread. Wealthy Europeans were eating so much sugar in the sixteenth century that their teeth turned black.

△ DENTAL INSTRUMENTS from the Middle Ages, probably used on rich people. Ordinary people had teeth pulled at the fair.

▽ 19TH-CENTURY DENTURES made of human teeth, gold, and ivory.

△ BEFORE the 19th century there was no dental profession, so many kinds of people would offer to pull out teeth.

△ HORACE WELLS tried to extract a tooth painlessly using anesthetic, but his patient groaned and the spectators were unconvinced.

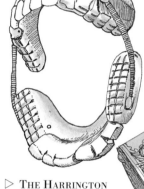

▷ THE HARRINGTON "ERADO" clockwork dentist's drill was made in 1864. It could work for as long as two minutes.

In the 150 years since anesthetics were first used in dentistry, the techniques and equipment involved have improved greatly. Today, dentists can even put back a tooth that has been knocked out accidentally. Techniques have been invented to stop teeth from decaying, to whiten them and to straighten them. Today it is difficult to tell whether people have dentures or not.

GUM DISEASE can be treated with an acrylic strip containing an antibiotic (right)

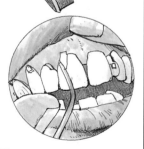

▽ IN 1991 Leeds University Dental Health Department developed a fluoride-releasing implant that will prevent teeth from decaying.

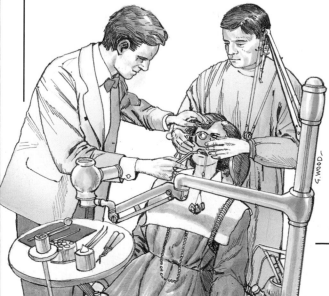

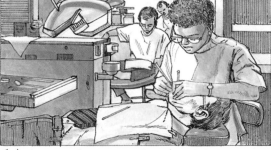

◁ △ A DENTIST'S OFFICE in the 1930s (left) looked different from those of today (above). Dentists now have access to increasingly sophisticated equipment such as ultrasound probes, which use high frequency sound waves to break up plaque.

MEDICINE AND WAR

△ "FLYING AMBULANCES" rescued soldiers from the battlefield during the Napoleonic wars.

△ NAVAL SURGEONS in the 18th century worked hard during battles, performing amputations and patching up the wounded as best they could. The floor of the operating bay was painted red so that the blood was not so obvious.

THROUGHOUT HISTORY, men who have fought in wars have had little in the way of medical care. Most armies included doctors but treatment was often reserved for officers. Although 18th-century ships had surgeons, sailors often died from infection because conditions were unhygienic.

In the Crimean War (1853-1856), when many soldiers were dying in filthy conditions because of the lack of medical care, there was a public outcry. Florence Nightingale was asked to go to the Crimea to care for the wounded – the first time that women had been allowed to nurse in the British Army.

△ FLORENCE NIGHTINGALE reformed nursing care, and is considered the founder of modern nursing.

▽ INSIDE a British ambulance train in northern France in 1918.

▷ MARY SEACOLE, a West Indian who traveled to the Crimea to nurse soldiers on the battlefield.

▷ A TRENCH HOSPITAL in World War I. They were often unhygienic, lacked sanitation, and were infested with rats. All trench hospitals were temporary – if the front line moved they often had to be abandoned.

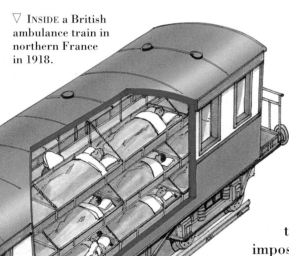

Medical care given to many war casualties was inadequate until recently. In World War I (1914-1918), the worst casualties were evacuated from the front. Trench hospitals were set up on the battlefield to give immediate treatment, although it was sometimes impossible to provide anything more than first aid. In World War II (1939-1945) scientists developed antibiotics and these were used successfully to treat the Allied forces. Since then, the medical profession has developed many techniques to help men and women wounded by modern weapons. Emergency teams can treat the wounded on the spot, and surgery to replace lost limbs and plastic surgery for burn victims is practiced throughout the world.

▽ IN WORLD WAR I the need for nurses was so great that untrained women were allowed to work alongside those with training. They were called the Voluntary Aid Detachments.

DRUGS

THE PERIOD between the end of World War I in 1918 and the end of World War II in 1945 saw many medical developments, especially in the discovery of new drugs, sometimes called "magic bullets" because of their seemingly magical healing qualities. In the early 1920s, Charles Best and Frederick Banting were working at the University of Toronto when they discovered that an extract made from the pancreas could control the high blood sugar that occurred in people with diabetes. The extract, insulin, was given successfully to a human patient in February 1922. Insulin gave new hope to millions of diabetics.

△ PAUL EHRLICH (*left*) and Sahachiro Hata (*right*) discovered the first drug that was effective against an infectious disease. They found in Salvarsan 606 a magic bullet that would kill the microorganism that caused syphilis but did not harm human tissue.

△ GERHARD DOMAGK discovered a magic bullet that could kill the bacteria that caused blood poisoning. He called it Prontosil.

◁ BANTING AND BEST studied dogs with diabetes. They found that a dog's symptoms disappeared when it was given an extract made from the pancreas, the organ in the body that releases digestive juices and also produces insulin. Today insulin is made on a large scale by bacteria that have been genetically engineered to produce human insulin molecules.

△ ALEXANDER FLEMING (*above*) discovered penicillin, but was not involved in the work that later made it available as a medicine.

△ FLEMING noticed that penicillin-producing mold killed bacteria. The application of his observation led to a cure for infection.

△ HOWARD FLOREY and his team did the work that led to penicillin being available as a treatment during the early 1940s.

△ FLOREY injected lethal doses of bacteria into 8 mice. He then treated 4 of them with penicillin; they were cured, the rest died.

△ SEVERAL MONTHS LATER Alexander Fleming visited Florey and his team at Oxford to discuss their success with penicillin.

In 1929, Alexander Fleming noticed that mold on one of his plates of bacteria was killing the germs around it. Ten years later, another scientist, Howard Florey, extracted pure penicillin from the mold juice; it was given to a patient for the first time in 1940. The patient's condition improved with the treatment but he died when the penicillin ran out. During World War II the extraction of penicillin was improved and by 1945 this "magic bullet" was available to treat Allied troops in Europe.

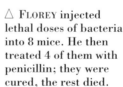

△ PENICILLIN was first made in bedpans, which were found to be a good shape to encourage the growth of mold.

▷ THE FIRST TRIAL of penicillin on a patient with a severe infection.

First human trial of penicillin. Patient given sulfonamide, early anti-infection drug. No effect.

Boils on face and scalp lanced to release pus.

Blood transfusion. Patient very ill with fever.

First dose of penicillin given. Improvement after 24 hours.

Great improvement but penicillin begins to run out.

Penicillin runs out. Patient dies within a month.

△ THE DRUGSTORE became a familiar landmark in the United States. As well as selling prescription medicines it was also a social center where people could buy ice cream sundaes and sodas.

◁ THE 1930s saw the start of a craze for health: people began to exercise and played more sports.

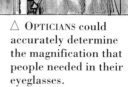

△ OPTICIANS could accurately determine the magnification that people needed in their eyeglasses.

△ X-RAY EQUIPMENT in the 1930s enabled doctors to see broken bones, tumors, gallstones and TB infection in the lungs.

▷ DISFIGURING INJURIES suffered by airmen in World War II required sophisticated surgical techniques. Archibald Melndoe and his team of plastic surgeons are shown at work (right).

The years between the two world wars saw advances in other areas of medicine. Opticians and dentists became more skilled and treatment more sophisticated. The use of X-rays to detect broken bones and large tumors became common. Several vitamins were identified and French doctors developed successful vaccines against tetanus and diphtheria, common infections that could be killers.

In 1932 the Nobel Prize for Medicine was awarded to the two doctors who discovered the neuron – the cell that makes up the nerves and the brain. Surgical techniques also improved and plastic surgery helped many soldiers who were disfigured in World Wars I and II.

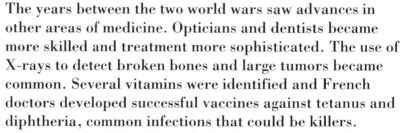

▽ THIS 1930S HOSPITAL is built on three floors and has an integral elevator to make the transport of patients easier. It has several wards, operating rooms, kitchens, bathrooms, examination rooms, a post-mortem room, a small chapel, and numerous storerooms for medical supplies and medicines. Nurses attending to the patients are shown in uniforms typical of the time.

HOSPITAL CARE

FROM THE 1930s TO THE 1950s, hospital care for the sick and injured became much more organized. In Britain in 1948 hospital care was revolutionized by the establishment of the National Health Service. The aim of the NHS was to provide free medical care for everyone in Britain, regardless of their social position, by the massive government funding of hospitals and NHS medical staff. The idea of a health service received much opposition from the British Medical Association when it was first introduced, but was later accepted when it began to benefit both patients and doctors.

△ ANEURIN BEVAN, then British minister for health, visiting an NHS hospital in 1948.

△ A 1940S CARTOON making fun of the NHS. The NHS remains controversial today.

A typical 1930s hospital was efficiently run and effectively laid out. The large open wards were light and airy and separate wards were provided for men and women, children, and the elderly. The children's ward on the top floor of this hospital has illustrated stories on its wall tiles to keep the children amused.

▽ BY THE 1930s nursing had become an accepted profession for women, but few women qualified as doctors.

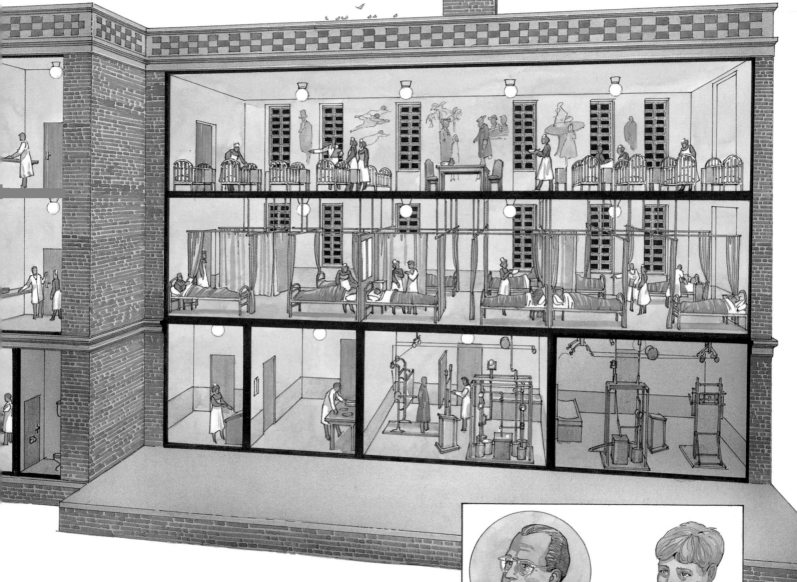

Polio is a viral disease that attacks the nerves. Before improved sanitation and better living conditions were introduced in the early twentieth century, most children were exposed to polio at an early age and became immune to it. Children infected later, at the age of four or five, became very ill. Many suffered temporary or permanent paralysis, in which case they had to spend some time in an artificial breathing machine called an iron lung (*shown lower right*). A polio vaccine was invented in 1953, and polio is now rare in developed countries.

△ ▽ IN 1953 Jonas Salk (*left*) developed a polio vaccine given by injection, which was replaced in 1957 by the Sabin oral vaccine, taken on a sugar lump (*right*). *Below*, an iron lung.

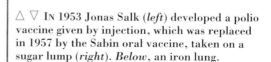

PREGNANCY AND CHILDBIRTH

THROUGHOUT HISTORY WOMEN have endured childbirth without much medical help. Help during delivery was usually provided by other women, who were the predecessors of today's midwives. Many women and babies died during childbirth. In the late nineteenth century anesthetics were introduced to help a mother with the pain, and trained midwives began to practice in the early twentieth century. This century has seen improvements in medical care in developed countries. A woman is now checked throughout her pregnancy, and tests and scans can tell when something is wrong with the fetus. Painkillers can be given during labor and intensive care is on hand for emergencies. In recent years, however, many women have taken the view that doctors interfere too much with childbirth. There is now a movement back to "natural childbirth," which rejects the use of drugs and tests during birth.

In the developing world, the rate of infant death is still high and many mothers give birth in conditions as primitive as those of two thousand years ago.

△ HATHOR was one of the Egyptian goddesses of childbirth.

▽ ROMAN MOTHERS usually had many children. Childbirth would have been a painful process and only two or three of her children might have lived to their teens.

△ ROMAN COUPLES tried alum, vinegar, and brine as contraceptives but none worked well.

▷ THIS PAINTING from Leipzig in 1400 showed the medieval perception of pregnancy.

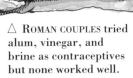

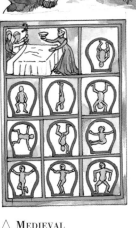

△ MEDIEVAL ILLUSTRATION showing the positions of the baby in the womb.

◁ A VASE from the Incas of South America showing a woman about to give birth.

△ A WOODCUT from 1500 showing a birth. The stars indicate that the baby's horoscope will be told at birth.

The survival rate of women after childbirth has improved dramatically during the last hundred years. A better diet, cleaner living conditions, and antibiotics have all played a part.

△ IVORY MODELS of pregnant women from 17th-century Nuremberg. They were 6-7 inches (16-18 cm) long and could be taken apart and reassembled.

▷ THIS ILLUSTRATION of a woman giving birth by Cesarean section (the baby is cut from her body rather than being pushed out) appeared in a 16-century book.

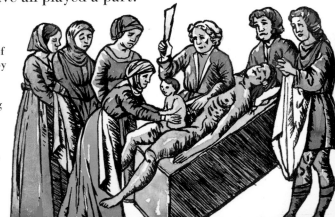

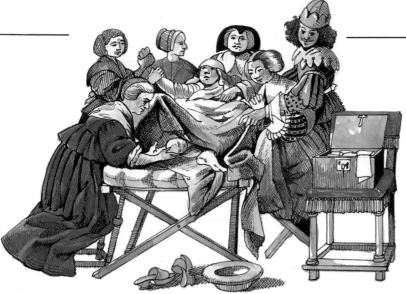

△ ENGRAVING by Abraham Bosse (1602-1676) showing a woman in childbirth in the 17th century.

The woman is lying on her back, supported by four women who may be relatives or friends, with the midwife receiving the baby as it is born. The man in attendance is probably a doctor.

Women have always used different positions when giving birth. Before the seventeenth century many women used birthing chairs or simply squatted as they pushed the baby out. It later became common for a woman to lie on her back. Since the 1970s, however, many women have rebelled against being told what to do by (often) male doctors and have started to use birthing cushions and chairs and squatting positions again.

THESE 18TH-CENTURY FORCEPS were used for difficult births.

▷ BABY'S BOTTLE. 18th century.

◁ AMERICAN INDIAN WOMEN gave birth in different positions. In some tribes the woman gave birth alone while in others helpers would support her.

◁ THE HUNGARIAN Ignaz Semmelweiss (1818-1865) found that fewer women died from fever after the birth if doctors washed their hands between examining different women in labor. But his ideas were not taken up until after his death.

△ A 17TH-CENTURY BIRTHING CHAIR (left) and a 19th-century baby walker (right).

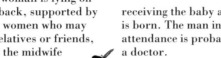

▷ IN 1902 a Midwives Act was passed in Britain, which made it compulsory for all midwives to be trained. Right, a midwife before and, far right, a midwife trained after the Act.

▽ SINCE THE 1970S babies born before they are fully developed have had a better chance of survival because of incubators. Today many hospitals have special baby units with incubators and other technology to save the lives of babies who may weigh only 1-2 lb (500g) at birth.

△ A WOMAN from Victorian high society gave birth in luxurious surroundings, with the best medical care.

▷ MOTHERS are now being encouraged to breast-feed because it is the most natural and nutritious way to feed babies. Breast-feeding gives mother and baby a good opportunity to bond together.

▽ BREASTMILK protects babies from infection and allergies because it contains antibodies from the mother's blood.

ALTERNATIVE MEDICINE

UNTIL THE 1850s all medicine involved treatments that are now called alternative or complementary – herbalism, water therapy, acupuncture, fasting, and bloodletting. Today, alternative medicine is a term used to describe medical treatments that are not based on the science-centered medicine that has become widespread since the 1850s. Alternative therapies include homeopathy, acupuncture, water therapy, herbalism, reflexology, and many more. Some people use alternative treatments as their only form of medicine while others use them alongside modern therapies. Many alternative treatments are claimed to have dramatic effects and many people swear by them, but we do not know for sure whether they actually work.

△ JEAN MARTIN CHARCOT (1825-1893) used the technique of hypnosis on patients at the Salpetrière Hospital in Paris.

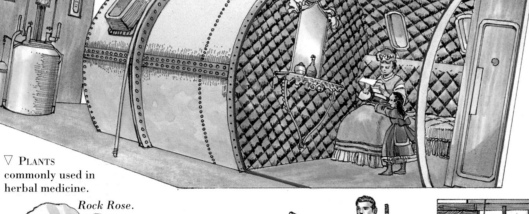

△ FATHER SEBASTIAN KNEIPP (1821-1897) devised a cure based on water, fresh air, sunshine, and walking barefoot in the snow.

◁ AEROTHERAPY in Milan in the 1870s. Chemically purified air was blown at high pressure into a cylindrical room to "cleanse" the patient's lungs and airways.

▽ PLANTS commonly used in herbal medicine.

Rock Rose.

Centaury.

Impatiens.

▽ HERBAL MEDICINE dates back thousands of years and has been used throughout history. Herbs are still the main form of treatment for illness in many poorer countries today. Herbalists stress the importance of using the whole, balanced plant as treatment.

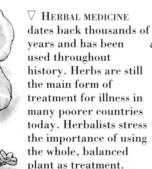

△ 19TH-CENTURY STEAM CABINET BATH. Steam was pumped into the closed cabinet, giving an "enclosed sauna."

Chicory.

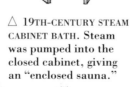

Water violet.

△ THE DOUCHE BATH, or cold shower, 1855. This was thought to be good for nervous complaints.

△ IN A MODERN DOUCHE, jets of water at high pressure are directed at the patient.

◁ WRAPPING PATIENTS in wet cloth. A 19th-century shoulder pack and chest compress (*left*), and a T-pack and trunk pack (*right*).

34

Reflexology is thought to have
first been used in China, where
it existed alongside acupuncture.
It was also common in Kenya and among
American Indian tribes. The theory of reflexology
is that each area of the body is linked to a reflex in
the foot and the position of each reflex can be mapped. A
trained reflexologist can massage the area of the foot
relating to the part of the body affected by illness and can
ease the symptoms. People of all ages are said to benefit
from reflexology; babies and young children need very
gentle massage and show rapid improvement, but older
people need several treatments before results are seen.

△ POINTS
on the feet that
correspond to affected
parts of the body feel
tender to touch.

△ THIS REFLEXOLOGIST
is massaging an area of
the feet that relates to
the diaphragm to relax
it and allow the
patient to breathe
more easily.

△ SAMUEL HAHNEMANN,
(1755-1843) founder of
homeopathy, which
treats illness using
dilute substances.

1. HOMEOPATHIC MEDICINES are
made from natural
ingredients. These are
treated and filtered to give a
raw medicine called "mother
tincture."

2. One drop of tincture is then
added to 99 drops of alcohol
to dilute it 100 times.
Homeopathy states that the
more diluted a medicine is,
the more effective it is.

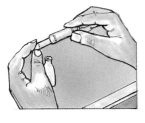

3. The diluted solution may be
diluted again and again,
each time by adding one
drop of solution to 99 drops
of alcohol. The solution is
then put into a vial.

△ LOURDES attracts
many people who hope
to be healed by faith.
Below, the laying on of
hands is part of healing.

The Chinese first became interested in
puncturing the skin as a treatment
when they noticed that soldiers
wounded by arrows sometimes
recovered from illnesses they had had
for many years. Today, by inserting
needles at points along channels, or
meridians, an acupuncturist believes
he or she is rebalancing the forces of
light and dark (yin and yang) within
the patient's body.

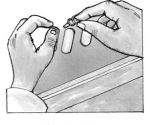

4. The vial is shaken on a
special machine to
transfer the "energy" of
the drop of medicine to
the whole solution.

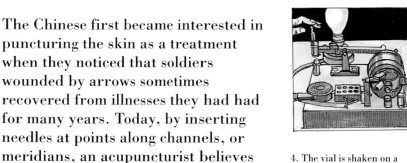

5. A small amount of the
final solution is added to
sugar tablets. Each tablet
is believed to receive some
of the energy from the
solution.

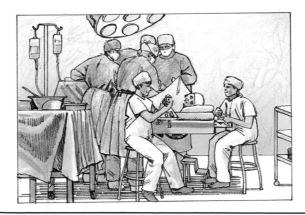

◁ ▷ ACUPUNCTURE has
been used as an
anesthetic in China
(*left*). It has been
claimed that patients
are awake throughout
surgery but feel no pain
and suffer no side
effects. A 19th-century
chart (*right*) showing
the acupuncture needle
points along one of the
14 meridians in the
human body.

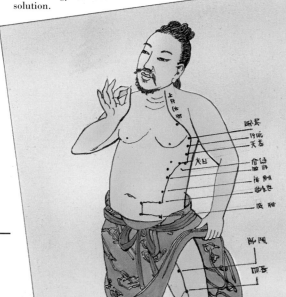

THE 1950S AND 1960S

△ ▽ FRANCIS CRICK (*above*, born 1916) and James Watson (*below*, born 1928) were awarded the Nobel Prize for their discovery that the structure of DNA was a double helix.

ONE OF THE MOST IMPORTANT MEDICAL DISCOVERIES of this century was made by four scientists in Britain: James Watson, Francis Crick, Maurice Wilkins, and Rosalind Franklin. They discovered the chemical structure of DNA, the genetic material present in all living organisms. This finding was the start of a new branch of medical science, molecular biology, from which techniques such as genetic therapy and cloning developed. The research was a sort of race: Crick and Watson worked together in one team while Wilkins and Franklin worked in another. Crick and Watson published their findings first, but Wilkins was later awarded the Nobel Prize jointly with them in 1962. Franklin had already died of cancer and could not be honored with them, because a Nobel Prize cannot be awarded after a person has died.

△ INTRODUCED in the 1960s, the birth control pill is an effective form of contraception. The side effects of long-term use are still not fully understood.

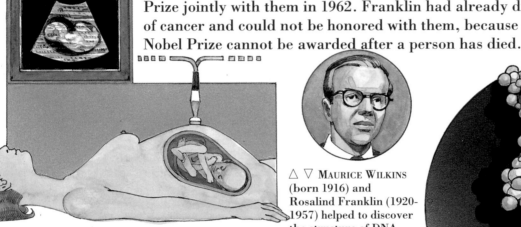

▽ A KIDNEY DIALYSIS machine is actually an artificial kidney. The patient's blood is pumped through a kind of filter inside it so that poisonous waste can be removed.

△ ULTRASOUND was developed from sonar used on World War II submarines. It was first used to scan pregnant women in the late 1950s.

△ ▽ MAURICE WILKINS (born 1916) and Rosalind Franklin (1920-1957) helped to discover the structure of DNA.

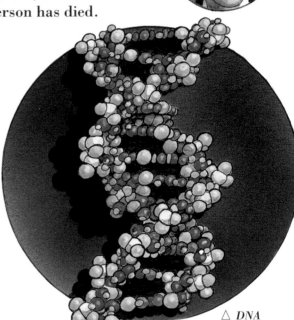

△ DNA

▷ MAMMOGRAPHY, first used in 1967, helps to identify potentially dangerous lumps in women's breasts, allowing them to be treated quickly.

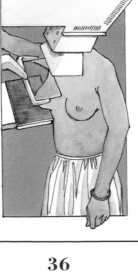

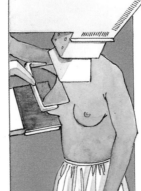

In the 1960s, doctors began to better understand the causes of cancer. Scanning techniques to screen for cancers were developed and used in hospitals for the first time. As well as an X-ray machine (mammograph) that identifies lumps in the breast, the CT body scanner, which can visualize the body in "slices," was invented. The first clinical prototype of the CT scanner was installed at the Atkinson Morley's Hospital in London in 1971.

△ CHRISTIAAN BARNARD (born 1922) performed the first successful human heart transplant in December 1967.

△ LOUIS WASHKANSKY, who was to receive the transplant, was admitted into the hospital and carefully examined before the operation.

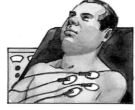

△ LOUIS'S KIDNEY FUNCTION was checked, his liver was studied, his heart pattern was plotted, and his lungs were X-rayed.

▷ A DOCTOR'S BAG from 1969.

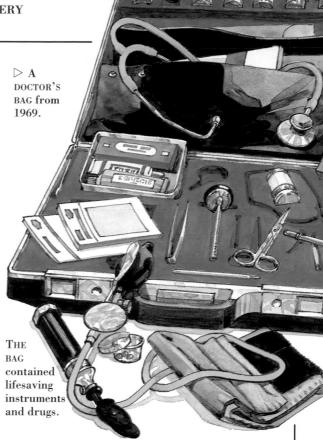

△ SWABS were taken to identify the bacteria living in Louis's skin, nose, throat, and rectum, in case they caused infection later.

△ HE WAS WASHED repeatedly in strong disinfectant and every utensil in the operating room was boiled.

△ DOCTORS waited for a donor heart – from someone dying with an uninjured heart.

THE BAG contained lifesaving instruments and drugs.

A heart transplant operation takes several hours. The patient is hooked up to a heart-lung machine so that he or she will stay alive while the heart is removed. The machine pumps oxygenated blood around the body so that the patient's brain and tissues are not harmed through lack of blood.

| In a heart transplant, the donor's heart (*above*) is removed. | The recipient's heart is then cut out, leaving only the top part remaining. | The new heart is stitched onto the remainder of the recipient's | heart, first on one side, then the other (*above left and right*). | The heart is cleared of air and final stitching is completed. |

Louis Washkansky, the first patient to receive a heart transplant, died after eighteen days. Techniques have greatly improved and now seventy-five percent of heart transplant patients are alive a year later. Heart and lung transplants have also been done, and sometimes patients with cystic fibrosis receive a new heart and lungs. Their own heart (which is usually healthy) is then transplanted into another patient. This is called a domino transplant.

▽ BY THE END of the 1960s many lifesaving drugs were being mass-produced.

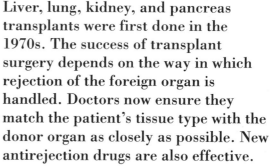

Liver, lung, kidney, and pancreas transplants were first done in the 1970s. The success of transplant surgery depends on the way in which rejection of the foreign organ is handled. Doctors now ensure they match the patient's tissue type with the donor organ as closely as possible. New antirejection drugs are also effective.

Diamond-headed scalpel.

1970 TO 1979

SMALLPOX VACCINATION is one of the greatest success stories in the history of medicine. Pioneered by Edward Jenner in 1796, the vaccination continued to be improved throughout the nineteenth and twentieth centuries. In 1979 the World Health Organization declared that smallpox had been wiped out throughout the world. The last recorded case of smallpox to result from a person-to-person infection was in Somalia in 1977, but a British scientist caught the disease from a laboratory accident in 1978. She died and now the security measures for storing the smallpox virus in laboratories are much tighter.

△ THIS GAS-DRIVEN smallpox vaccination gun, which uses no needles, was developed in the 1970s.

△ HIP JOINT SURGERY was given a germ-free environment with the Charnley-Howarth Body Exhaust System.

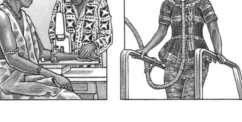

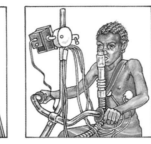

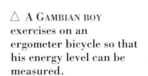

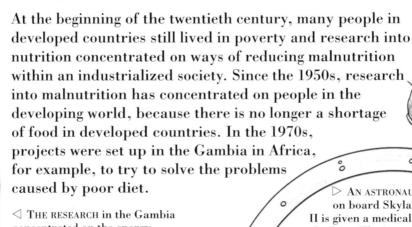

△ THIS GAMBIAN MOTHER is having the mineral content of her bone measured to find out if it contains the proper level of calcium.

△ A BREAST-FEEDING GAMBIAN MOTHER is being tested to find out how much energy she uses while walking.

△ A GAMBIAN BOY exercises on an ergometer bicycle so that his energy level can be measured.

△ THE CHARNLEY-HOWARTH ENCLOSURE provided one operating room within another to ensure a sterile area.

At the beginning of the twentieth century, many people in developed countries still lived in poverty and research into nutrition concentrated on ways of reducing malnutrition within an industrialized society. Since the 1950s, research into malnutrition has concentrated on people in the developing world, because there is no longer a shortage of food in developed countries. In the 1970s, projects were set up in the Gambia in Africa, for example, to try to solve the problems caused by poor diet.

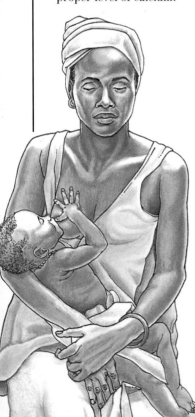

◁ THE RESEARCH in the Gambia concentrated on the energy requirements of women who were pregnant or who had just had babies. The new mothers were trying to restart work and breast-feed their babies on a very poor diet. Their underweight babies were not growing properly. Nutritionists developed high-energy biscuits for the mothers to eat so that they could produce enough breastmilk to feed their babies.

▷ AN ASTRONAUT on board Skylab II is given a medical checkup. The increase in space travel in the 1970s led to a new branch of medicine to deal with special problems.

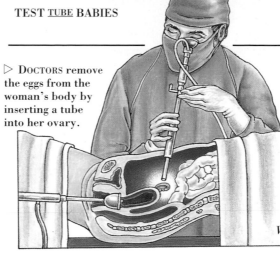

△ WHEN A COUPLE who want children seem to be infertile, various tests are done on both of them. Doctors might then recommend the couple try to have a "test-tube" baby.

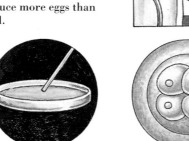

△ THE FIRST STEP in this technique – called "in vitro fertilization" – is to give the woman hormones called gonadotrophins to stimulate her ovaries to produce more eggs than usual.

▷ DOCTORS remove the eggs from the woman's body by inserting a tube into her ovary.

▽ THE EGGS are then placed into a shallow dish (not actually a test tube). The eggs are kept in a special fluid until they are mixed with the sperm.

Woman's egg.

△ IN THE MEANTIME the sperm are prepared so that they are able to fertilize the eggs. Special chemicals are used to make the sperm "ripen."

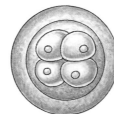

△ THE EGGS AND SPERM are mixed in the dish and incubated between 42 and 72 hours. If an egg is fertilized it begins to divide into a tiny ball of 8 cells.

△ THIS BALL OF CELLS is now called a pre-embryo and is at the stage when it would normally implant into the wall of the mother's womb.

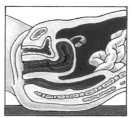

△ ONE OR MORE PRE-EMBRYOS are introduced into the woman's womb. Drug therapy has prepared her womb lining so that it is ready to accept the egg.

△ IF AN EMBRYO IMPLANTS in the wall of the womb the woman becomes pregnant. But so far in vitro fertilization has had a low success rate.

Infertility can be very distressing for a couple who want to have children. In 1978 the first "test-tube" baby, Louise Brown, was born. The technique is actually called "in vitro fertilization" because the fertilization stage takes place outside the mother's body in a glass dish (the Latin phrase for "in glass" is "in vitro"). This achievement of modern medicine represented many years of research by Patrick Steptoe and Robert Edward. During their research they discovered many things about the normal process of pregnancy that had not been known before. Hundreds of couples have been helped to have families. But the technique has led to some ethical concerns, for instance about surrogate motherhood and embryo research.

△ A SURGICAIR MATTRESS and a microclimator are used to treat people with severe burns.

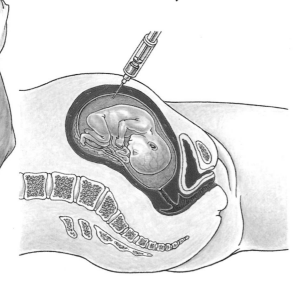

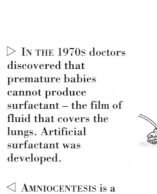

▷ IN THE 1970s doctors discovered that premature babies cannot produce surfactant – the film of fluid that covers the lungs. Artificial surfactant was developed.

◁ AMNIOCENTESIS is a test in which a needle is inserted into a pregnant woman's abdomen and some of the fluid that surrounds the baby is taken and tested to detect whether the baby has a genetic disorder.

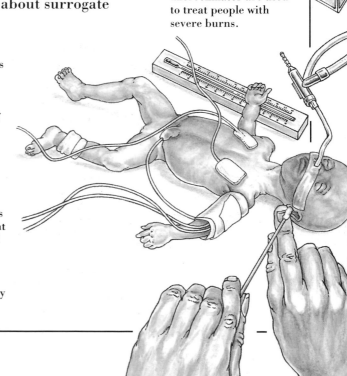

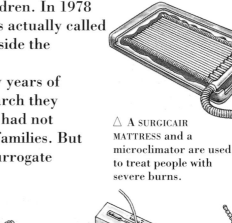

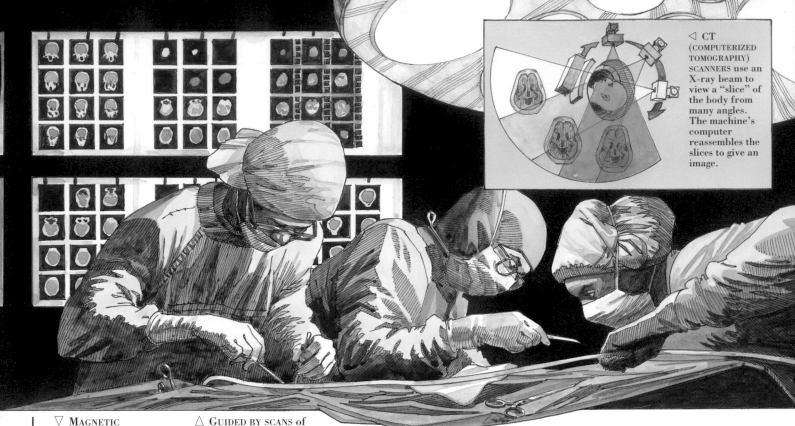

CT (COMPUTERIZED TOMOGRAPHY) SCANNERS use an X-ray beam to view a "slice" of the body from many angles. The machine's computer reassembles the slices to give an image.

▽ MAGNETIC RESONANCE IMAGING – a scan that uses magnetism instead of X-rays to detect a tumor.

△ GUIDED BY SCANS of the patient's brain, these surgeons implant a tube to drain excess fluid inside the skull.

SURGERY

SURGERY HAS ADVANCED ENORMOUSLY since the major discoveries of anesthesia and aseptic techniques in the nineteenth century. In the 1960s, 1970s, and 1980s many technical breakthroughs were made, making surgery in the 1980s unbelievably effective at solving all sorts of problems that were previously fatal, such as some kinds of cancer. As well as improvements in the skills involved in surgery, increased medical technology has allowed surgeons to "see" accurate three-dimensional pictures of the inside of the body before they cut into it. Ultrasound, Magnetic Resonance Imaging, Digital Subtraction Angiography, CT scanning, and PET scanning can each be used to give different images of internal organs, which surgeons can use as "maps" as they operate. In one operation in the 1980s, a young boy had a tumor removed from his brain.

Without detailed images showing the exact position of the lump, he would almost certainly have died.

▽ A DIGITAL BIPLANE ANGIOSCOPE can show a three-dimensional moving picture of the heart.

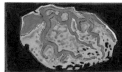

△ DSA (Digital Subtraction Angiography) can show the position of a blocked artery.

▷ A PET (Positron Emission Tomography) scanner can show if a heart is receiving the normal supply of blood.

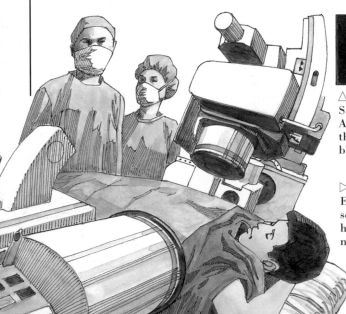

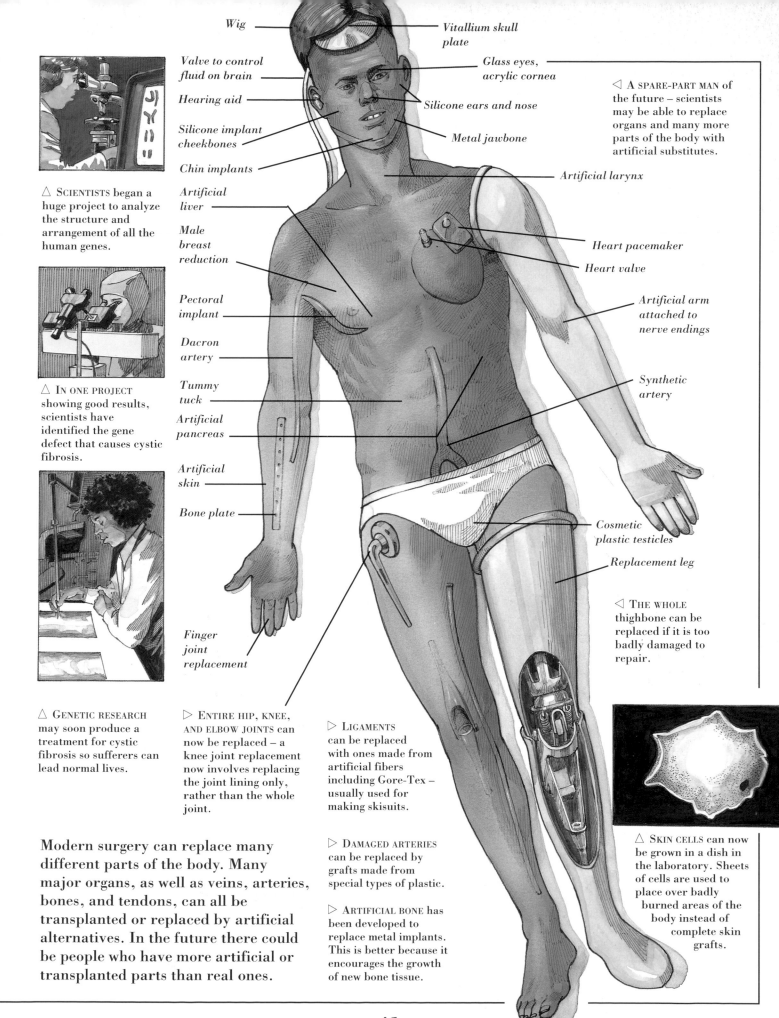

Wig

Vitallium skull plate

Valve to control fluid on brain

Glass eyes, acrylic cornea

Hearing aid

Silicone ears and nose

Silicone implant cheekbones

Metal jawbone

Chin implants

Artificial liver

Artificial larynx

Male breast reduction

Heart pacemaker

Heart valve

Pectoral implant

Dacron artery

Artificial arm attached to nerve endings

Tummy tuck

Artificial pancreas

Synthetic artery

Artificial skin

Bone plate

Cosmetic plastic testicles

Replacement leg

Finger joint replacement

△ SCIENTISTS began a huge project to analyze the structure and arrangement of all the human genes.

△ IN ONE PROJECT showing good results, scientists have identified the gene defect that causes cystic fibrosis.

△ GENETIC RESEARCH may soon produce a treatment for cystic fibrosis so sufferers can lead normal lives.

◁ A SPARE-PART MAN of the future – scientists may be able to replace organs and many more parts of the body with artificial substitutes.

◁ THE WHOLE thighbone can be replaced if it is too badly damaged to repair.

▷ ENTIRE HIP, KNEE, AND ELBOW JOINTS can now be replaced – a knee joint replacement now involves replacing the joint lining only, rather than the whole joint.

▷ LIGAMENTS can be replaced with ones made from artificial fibers including Gore-Tex – usually used for making skisuits.

▷ DAMAGED ARTERIES can be replaced by grafts made from special types of plastic.

▷ ARTIFICIAL BONE has been developed to replace metal implants. This is better because it encourages the growth of new bone tissue.

△ SKIN CELLS can now be grown in a dish in the laboratory. Sheets of cells are used to place over badly burned areas of the body instead of complete skin grafts.

Modern surgery can replace many different parts of the body. Many major organs, as well as veins, arteries, bones, and tendons, can all be transplanted or replaced by artificial alternatives. In the future there could be people who have more artificial or transplanted parts than real ones.

41

MEDICINE TODAY

MODERN MEDICINE is highly sophisticated, and diseases that have caused pain and death for many generations can now be treated successfully. In the developed world a person born today can expect to live to eighty. But there is still disease: cancer and heart disease are the two most common causes of death and AIDS (Acquired Immune Deficiency Syndrome) is spreading. Scientists are trying to learn more about these diseases. Advances are currently being made in genetics, and some previously incurable diseases may soon have successful therapies. In the developing world medical priorities are different – many people still live in terrible poverty and infectious diseases are common. Malnutrition and AIDS are great threats to life there. Although many diseases can be prevented or cured, political barriers and lack of money can make modern medicine unattainable.

△ WHILE THE DEVELOPING WORLD has too little food, people in developed countries overeat, and eat too much fatty food. Some nutritionists' advice is to eat fresh food, including vegetables and fruit, instead.

△ AIDS is caused by the HIV virus, which is passed on by direct blood contact or by having unprotected sex. Using a condom and, for drug users, never sharing needles, are thought to reduce the risk of catching HIV.

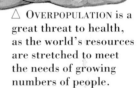

◁ ENDOSCOPY: a fiberoptic and camera with a tube are used to see inside the body.

△ OVERPOPULATION is a great threat to health, as the world's resources are stretched to meet the needs of growing numbers of people.

▽ THE WORLD HEALTH ORGANIZATION believes that medical treatment for all people should be available when they need it.

▷ SMALL AMOUNTS of alcohol numb nerve cells and slow their messages to the body. Larger amounts affect centers responsible for vision, balance, and judgement. Excessive drinking can cause unconsciousness and death.

SMOKING is known to cause throat and lung cancer. Almost 150,000 Americans die every year from lung cancer and the majority are smokers.

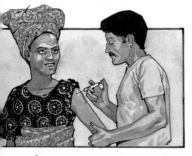

▷ HEAVY DRINKING can damage the liver so badly that is stops working.

◁ SMOKING WHILE PREGNANT can cause miscarriage. Women who smoke while pregnant may have underweight babies.

▽ EDUCATING WOMEN in developing countries about health, diet, and contraception is now a priority – if they are educated they will want their children to be educated too.

▷ THE FIRST GLASS of alcohol passes to the stomach and then to the small intestine, where it is rapidly absorbed into the bloodstream. In a few minutes it affects the brain. But taken sensibly, an alcoholic drink can be a pleasure that some doctors think may help to prevent heart disease.

◁ EVEN MODERATE DRINKING can affect an unborn baby. Children born to mothers who drank only a few glasses of wine per week during pregnancy have been born with fetal alcohol syndrome.

Liver

Intestines

Fetus

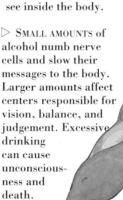

△ THE GREENHOUSE EFFECT occurs when pollutants such as carbon dioxide and methane build up in the atmosphere and act like greenhouse glass, keeping more heat in than is let out.

△ CARBON DIOXIDE is a by-product of some types of electricity production. Cars also emit carbon dioxide.

△ METHANE is produced by rotting garbage and by cows when they digest grass.

△ CUTTING DOWN rain forests means there are fewer trees left to absorb carbon dioxide.

THE FUTURE

The main concern of medicine in the next decades could be prevention rather than cure. Some diseases are known to have environmental causes – lung cancer is linked to heavy smoking, and heart disease can be linked to diet. Vaccines will be made better – soon it will be possible to transport them in hot climates without refrigeration. Scientists are working on a vaccine for AIDS. More emphasis may also be placed on treating the problems of the planet so that the people living on it can avoid illness linked to pollution and overpopulation. It is likely that the pace of discovery will be fast and one discovery will lead on to others. It is impossible to predict what medicine will be able to do in a hundred years' time, but it is bound to be beyond our wildest dreams.

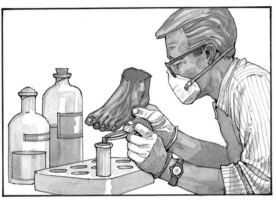

△ WITH THE NEW DNA TECHNOLOGY developed in the 1980s and 1990s, it may soon be possible to learn more about ancient civilizations by extracting and studying DNA from Egyptian mummies and bone fragments.

▽ VATS of liquid nitrogen for storing frozen human bodies.

▽ SOME PEOPLE are so convinced that medical science will find a cure for everything that they pay to have their bodies frozen after death. Their hope is that, eventually, technology will advance to a level where they can be defrosted, brought back to life and cured of the illness that killed them. This process is called cryogenics.

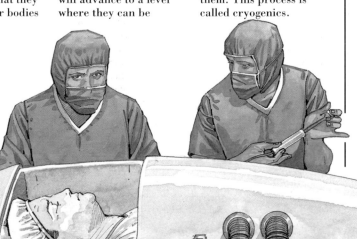

TIMELINE

Trepanning operation, c.20,000 B.C.

B.C.

c.2500 Operations performed in Egypt. Scenes of surgery carved on tombs of pharaohs.
c.2000 Code of Hammurabi – first code of practice in medicine – used in Babylon.
1550 Egyptian papyrus (document) written, probably a copy of a document 1,000 years older,

Clay jars to preserve internal organs of mummy

describing how to set broken bones. Another papyrus gives details of treatments for illness, including 700 medicines, plus diets, fasts, and massage.
1000 The Etruscans use false teeth. Chinese practice massage and acupuncture.
c.700 Patients are treated at the temples of the god Asclepius in Greece.
460-361 Hippocrates, founder of the Hippocratic oath and great medical teacher, lives in Greece.
384-322 Life of Aristotle, the second

Examining the urine in the Middle Ages

great Greek medical philosopher and teacher.

A.D.

130-201 Life of Galen, Roman doctor whose ideas on medicine are to last for centuries.
848-856 First recorded writings about the School of Salerno, the first medical school founded in Italy at the end of the Dark Ages. Many of the writings are in the form of highly illustrated manuscripts.
850-932 Life of Rhazes and peak of Islamic medicine.
1000 The Canon of Medicine written by Avicenna, another great figure in Islamic medicine. The work includes five volumes on Greek and Roman medicine that are used by doctors in Europe until the 17th century.
1137 St. Bartholomew's hospital founded by Rahere in London.
1270-1280 Eyeglasses first used by the Venetians to correct bad eyesight.
1319 First criminal prosecution for body snatching – the practice of stealing bodies from graves for anatomy classes.
1345 First pharmacy opens in London.
1348-1350 Black Death spreads across Europe, killing thousands of people. There is no treatment.
1452 The first professional association of midwives is founded in Regensburg, Germany.

1457 First medical publication, *Gutenburg Purgaton Calendar*, produced in Europe.
1493 Christopher Columbus discovers that Native Americans use tobacco as a medicine.
1500 The first recorded cesarean section performed on a living woman.
1505 Royal College of Surgeons is chartered in Edinburgh.
1514-1564 Life of Andreas Vesalius, great anatomist in Italy.

Rhazes examines a patient, ninth century

1518-1525 Smallpox reaches the Americas and causes an epidemic that affects the Aztec and Inca empires.
1540 English barbers and surgeons united as "Commonalty of the Barbers and Surgeons."
1545 Book by French surgeon Ambroise Paré recommends that wounds should not be treated with boiling oil, but with soothing ointments.
1549 Anatomy theater in Padua first used. Its special design allows every student to see the dissection clearly.
1561 Italian anatomist Gabriel Fallopius describes the female reproductive system. The Fallopian tubes are named after him.
1579 The first glass eyes are made.

1590 Compound microscope invented by Hans and Zacharias Janssen.
1614 The first study of metabolism published.
1628 English doctor William Harvey discovers that blood is circulated around the body.
1630s Treatment of malaria with the bark of the cinchona tree in Peru.
1647 Yellow fever taken by slaves from Africa to America.

1665, July to October Great Plague in Europe and Asia.
1683 Dutch merchant Antony van Leeuwenhoek describes and sketches bacteria, which he calls "animalcules," or little animals.
1701 Giacomo Pylarini reports the widespread practice of inoculation with smallpox pus to prevent people from getting the disease. Using this method he successfully inoculates three children against smallpox.
1714 Gabriel Fahrenheit invents a mercury thermometer, which, in the 19th century, becomes widely used in medicine. The Fahrenheit temperature scale was named after him.

1752 The Medical Society and St. George's hospital are founded in London.
1753 Scotsman James Lind describes how lemons and limes can cure scurvy. From 1795 all British sailors are made to drink lime juice, which is how the nickname "limey" came into use. Limes are later found to be rich in vitamin C and scurvy is classified as a disease caused by a vitamin deficiency.
1761 The Austrian Auenbrugger publishes his technique of tapping the chest wall of patients to detect chest disorders. The tone of the sound produced indicates whether the lungs are reasonably healthy or badly infected.
1774 German physician Anton Mesmer uses hypnotism to treat illness. The term "mesmerized" is later used to describe someone who is hypnotized, or who seems to be.
1775 A study of the health of chimney sweeps in London reveals that they develop cancer of the testicles at a much higher frequency than men doing other work. Soot is later identified as a risk factor.
1780 Benjamin Franklin invents bifocal lenses.
1791 The French

Renaissance surgery

physician Pinel advocates a more humane treatment of the mentally ill.
1796 Edward Jenner vaccinates James Phipps with pus from a cowpox sore to prevent him from getting smallpox.
1810 German doctor Samuel Hahnemann intoduces homeopathy.
1816 French doctor René Laënnec invents the stethoscope.
1831 American chemist Samuel Guthrie, German scientist Justus von Liebig, and French scientist Eugène Soubeiran all discover chloroform independently of each other during the same year.
1832 The Anatomy Act legalizes the sale of bodies for dissection in England, ending the

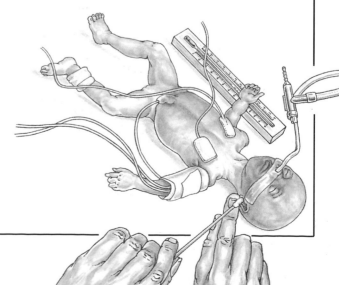

Anatomy lecture in Padua, 16th century

practice of body snatching.
1842 First use of the anesthetic ether.
1846 American dentist W. T. Morton uses ether in surgery.
1847 Hungarian doctor Ignaz Semmelweiss encourages surgeons to wash their hands between deliveries of babies, thus reducing

number of deaths from childbed fever.
1853 The hypodermic syringe is first used.
1854-1856 The Crimean War: Florence Nightingale sets up the field hospital at Scutari.
1860 French scientist Louis Pasteur demostrates presence of bacteria in air.
1865 Joseph Lister uses carbolic acid as an antiseptic spray to kill bacteria in his operating room, reducing the risk of death from infection after the operation.
1868 English doctor Sir Thomas Allbutt develops the clinical thermometer.
1871 Hammarsten discovers the role of fibrinogen in blood clotting.
1873 Bellevue Hospital in New York opens first school of nursing.
1882 German scientist Robert Koch discovers the organism that causes tuberculosis.
1885 Pasteur develops a vaccine for rabies.
1887 The first contact lens is developed in the United States.
1890 Behring treats a patient with diphtheria

with an antitoxin. This counteracts the effects of the toxin produced by the bacteria causing the disease.
1891 Halstend introduces rubber gloves for surgical operations.
1894 The bacterium that causes bubonic plague is discovered.
1895 Albert Calmette first uses serum against

snake poison.
1896 German physicist Wilhelm Roentgen first demonstrates X-rays in public. They become widely used in medicine to detect broken bones.
1899 Dreser first uses aspirin to give pain relief.
1900 Austrian doctor Karl Landsteiner discovers blood grouping.
1910 Salvarsan 606, the sulfonamide drug that is effective against bacterial infection, is first used.
1921 The Rorschach inkblot test is developed for the study of personality. Patients are asked to look at and interpret blots of ink.
1927 Ramon develops active immunization against tetanus and later diphtheria.
1928 English scientist Alexander Fleming discovers that a mold on one of his culture plates produces a substance that kills bacteria. He calls the substance penicillin.
1935 American scientist Wendall Stanley first describes a virus – the Tobacco Mosaic virus, which infects tomato plants.
1938 Florey, Chain, and others begin work on penicillin.
1939, September World War II begins – many advances made in sanitation, amputation, and in the treatment of wounds and infections.
1939 Penicillin first used to treat patients.
1940s The electron microscope allows viruses to be photographed for the first time.
1951 Scientists first realize the effect of fluoride on tooth decay.
1953 Crick and Watson, with the contributions of Franklin and Wilkins, work out that the structure of DNA is a

double helix.
1959 Beginning of space medicine and the study of how the physiology of the human body is affected by space travel and weightlessness.
1960s New and improved surgical instruments developed. Laser surgery introduced for skin grafting, cataract operations, and operations to remove tumors.
1966 Harry Meyer and Paul Parman develop a vaccine for German Measles.
1967 South African doctor Christiaan Barnard performs first heart transplant.
1971 The first computerized tomography scanner (CT scan) is introduced as a prototype.
1973 The MRI (magnetic resonance imager) scanner is introduced as a prototype.
1977 Two men in New York are diagnosed as having Kaposi's sarcoma – they are probably the earliest known victims of AIDS in the developed world. Last recorded case of smallpox found in the wild in Somalia.
1978 First test-tube baby, Louise Brown, is born.

Treatment of premature baby, present day

1981 AIDS is officially recognized as a disease. The search for a cure or a vaccine for AIDS begins.
1982 Eli Lilly and Company market human insulin that has been produced by genetically engineered bacteria.
1984 The first successful surgery is performed on a baby while it is still inside the womb.
1985 Lasers are first used to unclog blocked arteries.
1988 Scientists Louis Kunkel and Eric Hoffman announce the discovery of dystrophin, the protein missing in people with

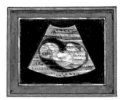

Ultrasound scan, present day

Duchenne muscular dystrophy. This leads to accurate diagnosis of the disease in its early stages.
1990s Huge worldwide project to sequence the entire human genome gets fully underway.

GLOSSARY

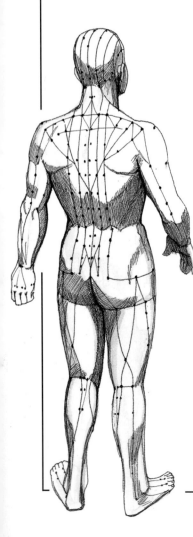

Acupuncture A type of Eastern medicine in which small needles are inserted into the skin to treat illness by restoring the natural energy balance of the body. It has been in use in China for at least four thousand years.

AIDS (Acquired Immune Deficiency Syndrome) A disease of the immune system that has only been recognized since the 1980s. It can take ten years to develop.

Anesthetic Drug that prevents a patient from feeling pain either by numbing part of the body (local anesthetic) or by putting that patient to sleep (general anesthetic).

Anatomy The branch of medicine that concentrates on the structure of the body. Dissection of dead bodies is an important part of anatomy.

Antibiotic Drug that can cure bacterial infections.

Antiseptic A chemical that kills bacteria outside the body.

Apothecary Old term for a pharmacist or chemist – a person who dispenses drugs.

Aseptic Sterile, bacteria-free.

Bacteria (singular Bacterium) Simple, single-cell organisms that are a major cause of human disease, although most bacteria are harmless and even beneficial to nature.

Bile Fluid secreted by the liver and stored in the gall bladder. It aids digestion.

Black Death Fatal disease that spread through Europe during the Middle Ages. It is also known as the Plague.

Cancer The growth of abnormal cells in the body, which can lead to death if not treated early. The term is used to describe a disease in which cells of the body divide uncontrollably. Cancers can spread through the body, and tumors, or lumps, can arise in any tissue.

Cesarean section An operation to remove a baby from its mother's womb when she has difficulty giving birth naturally.

Dentures False teeth.

DNA (deoxyribonucleic acid) The chemical that makes up the genetic material in every living cell.

Fetish An object believed to possess supernatural powers, which is often carried by witch doctors.

Fetal alcohol syndrome The damage caused to some unborn children when their mothers drink alcohol while pregnant.

Fetus A baby in the womb once its main adult features can be recognized, after about eight weeks.

HIV (Human Immunodeficiency Virus) The virus that causes AIDS.

Hypnosis A state of relaxed wakefulness, sometimes called a trance, when a person obeys suggestions very easily.

Lance To prick or cut open. It is commonly used to describe the opening of boils or sores to let out the pus.

Latrines Toilets.

Leprosy A disfiguring disease caused by a microorganism that was common in the Middle Ages, but which today is found mainly in the tropics.

Lockjaw A popular name for tetanus, a disease of the central nervous system. It is called lockjaw because it causes stiffness and muscular spasms, especially of the jaw.

Midwife A person who assists a woman in the delivery of her child.

Mummification The process of preparing a dead body for the afterlife, which was practiced in ancient Egypt. Mummification involved removing internal organs and preserving the body by wrapping it in linen bandages.

Piles A painful condition of the lower rectum, also called hemorrhoids.

Plastic surgery Surgery to rebuild damaged or disfigured parts of the body. Cosmetic surgery is a type of plastic surgery done purely to improve a person's appearance.

Poliomyelitis Disease of the nervous system that can lead to paralysis.

Psychiatry The branch of medicine that concentrates on mental illness.

Pulse The regular wave of blood in a person's artery as it is pumped by the heart.

Scurvy Illness that results when people do not eat enough vitamin C.

Smallpox Viral disease that is highly contagious and often fatal. Its symptoms (outward signs) are high fever and a severe rash, but its spread has been stopped by vaccination.

Sphygmomanometer Instrument that measures blood pressure. It is comprised of a cuff and a rubber bulb, and is used with a stethoscope.

Stethoscope An instrument that allows a doctor to hear activity within the body, in organs such as the heart and lungs.

Syphilis A disease usually caused by sexual contact, which can prove fatal if not treated.

Traction Putting force on a broken bone to make sure it is properly aligned when healing. Traction is usually carried out using weights on pulleys.

Trepanning The ancient practice of cutting a hole in the skull to relieve headaches or to release evil spirits.

Uroscopy The term used to describe the practice of examining the urine to diagnose illness.

Vaccine An extract of a disease-causing organism that activates the immune system against that organism. This protects people from developing the disease even if they come into contact with an infected person.

World Health Organization (WHO) A unit set up by the United Nations in 1948 to act as an information center about the health problems facing the world. The WHO carries out research, trains medical staff, and issues international health regulations.

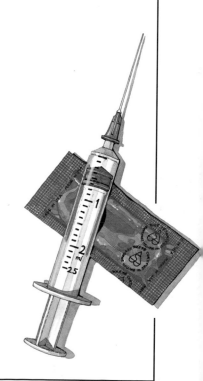

INDEX

PRINTED IN BELGIUM BY

INTERNATIONAL BOOK PRODUCTION